MW01063973

Angels in the Workplace

Angels in the Workplace

*Stories
and Inspirations
for Creating
a New World
of Work*

∞

Melissa Giovagnoli

JOSSEY-BASS
SAN FRANCISCO

Jossey-Bass books and products are available through most bookstores. To contact Jossey-Bass directly, call (888) 378-2537, fax to (800) 605-2665, or visit our website at www.josseybass.com.

Substantial discounts on bulk quantities of Jossey-Bass books are available to corporations, professional associations, and other organizations. For details and discount information, contact the special sales department at Jossey-Bass.

 Manufactured in the United States of America on Lyons Falls Turin Book. This paper is acid-free and 100 percent totally chlorine-free.

Library of Congress Cataloging-in-Publication Data

Giovagnoli, Melissa.
    Angels in the workplace: stories and inspirations for creating a new world of work / Melissa Giovagnoli. — 1st ed.
      p. cm.
    ISBN 0-7879-4369-X (acid-free paper)
    1. Psychology, Industrial—Religious aspects. 2. Angels. I. Title.
    HF5548.8.G53   1998
    650.1—ddc21   98–40100

FIRST EDITION
HB Printing   10 9 8 7 6 5 4 3 2 1

Contents

Preface

Why Angels?

Not only do 96 percent believe in God, most Americans also believe in: heaven, 90 percent; miracles, 79 percent; angels, 72 percent.

—*USA TODAY/*CNN GALLUP POLL

Angels are featured in Christianity, Judaism, Islam, and other religions. In countless Old and New Testament verses, we find angels performing their chief function—acting as God's messengers. Other religions, including Buddhism and Hinduism, mention angels throughout their scriptures as well.

—LIESL VAZQUEZ, *ANGELS IN OUR MIDST*

There is strong and growing interest in angels in our lives. For me, angels in the workplace represent a transcendence that offers all of us new meaning and understanding of purpose in our working lives, in the place where we spend the majority of our waking hours.

It is important at the outset to recognize that we all "work," whether in or out of the home, full-time or part-time, doing for-profit or not-for-profit work. Whenever we attempt to achieve an outcome different from our current condition,

---

In just a few of the cases, I've changed the names of the angels to protect confidentiality when needed.

we are working. Any mother or father taking care of children finds that the home is a work environment in which angel beliefs are no less important than they are in the familiar image of the workplace.

In this book, you will also find how important angel beliefs are to achieving work-family and work-life balance. The issue of balance is becoming increasingly important to men as well as women. A growing number of organizations are asking me to talk about it. In this book, I focus on balance from the perspective of taking time for yourself: getting quiet, to let the ceaseless activity of the mind settle so that you can see and hear more clearly who you really are. Once you are able to hear your unique voice, you become deeply aware of just how you fit in. You own who you really are and the purpose that only you can fulfill for the world—if you choose to own your purpose. In alignment with purpose, you activate a powerful catalyst to your spiritual growth.

In this book, you learn that work is one of the best catalysts for spiritual growth. Those who know how to turn work into a highly spiritual activity are better able to embrace the unlimited power of the divine. Whether your workplace has become unsupportive, or discouraging, or even fearful, you learn from others, just like yourself, that there is hope. Through the lives of people in every workplace environment, you gain support and insight for making your worklife work for you.

Further, by serving others you learn how angels make the kind of difference we so desperately need in our world today. It is this connection to serving that shows you the illuminated path toward the satisfaction you seek in the workplace, a path that any can travel. Mother Teresa and Princess Diana were just two of the many workplace angels who understand this potent connection to the divine. These two women realized that we each have a definite purpose in life and that our purpose always has something to do with serving others. Whereas these angels were outside the traditional workplace environment, this book shares stories from everyday angels coming from all walks of life—from executives to janitors. You learn that the peace and purpose so many of us seek in our everyday lives is indeed attainable.

In this book, I have the privilege of sharing many inspirational stories of people I call workplace angels, the truest of leaders forging a new world of work. This new world of work is your individually created divine space, where you are personally rewarded. Here you become your own best advocate for supporting the basic beliefs (faith, hope, charity, courage, truth, trust, and love) that make up the foundation for a new world of work. However, it is not realistic to believe you can create this new world without help. The stories and strategies in each section serve as guideposts to show you just how you can travel the path to an enlightened workplace.

The people in this book come from different religious backgrounds. My intent has always been to include and respect all spiritual beliefs. I use the word *God* throughout the book not to exclude but to refer to recognition of a divine source that speaks all of our languages. I believe this is essential to creating a new world of work.

If I offend anyone, I sincerely apologize. This book is about the journey to joy; it is about belonging, feeling connected to something bigger than yourself—something divine—that in turn helps you realize you are not alone.

May the beauty and the light of the angels showcased in this book cascade into your life like warm morning sunshine, and may God bless us, every one of us, as we work toward a better tomorrow.

∞

To Cindy, Cari, and Greg . . . to our victory

Acknowledgments

As with any successful book, it took a team of angels to achieve this finished product. I am thankful for the many wonderful souls who treated this book as if it were their own. They truly understand that no one can do it alone.

I would like first to thank Cedric Crocker, my editor, for his continuous excitement and support for this book. He enabled me to stay focused and filled with energy throughout the writing period. Thanks also to Cheryl Greenway, who was just as committed and responsive to the vision of the book. When it comes to angel teams, they don't get any better than the great production team at Jossey-Bass.

I would also like to thank my incredibly gifted outside editorial and research colleagues, Candy Gossling, Margo Pachona, Cindy Goodman, Jeri Sedlar, and Rick Miners, who were tireless in helping me locate angels and stay true to the seven beliefs of workplace angels. They are angels themselves.

This book would have blank pages if it were not for the many outstanding angels who shared their powerful stories. They have been catalysts for me every day to pay more attention to service as a lifetime vocation. (They are also personally recognized in the Resource section of this book.)

I also want to thank you, Dear Reader, for adding this work to your bookshelf. I have faith that you will use it as a tool to find the joy you so richly deserve, and that you will pass the joy on to as many others as possible.

Thanks also to the many clients, colleagues, and friends who have helped me build my belief in angels in the workplace—and in the "worldplace." Their regular support has been invaluable to me.

Finally, thank you to my wonderful family. Abraham Lincoln called upon each of us to look for the angels within ourselves; I didn't have to look too far to find angels among my family members.

The Author

Melissa Giovagnoli is a nationally known speaker and trainer, and the author of five other widely acclaimed, internationally sold books (including coauthorship of *The Power of Two*, recently released by Jossey-Bass) on the development of human potential. For more than eighteen years, she has worked with many of the world's leading organizations, assisting individuals and teams in building powerful workplace communities imbued with the seven principles she shares in this book. Her mission is to integrate the beliefs of powerful workplace angels within the workplace and out into what she calls the "worldplace." She is also the founder of Service Showcase, a twelve-year-old innovative management consulting and training organization located in suburban Chicago. Through her leadership, she has formed alliances with everyone from the federal government to schools to nonprofits and local organizations in her effort to get people collaborating to make a difference. She lives with her husband, Steve, and two sons, Graham and Gavin, in Schaumburg, Illinois.

Angels in the Workplace

Introduction

*The Seven Beliefs of Powerful
Workplace Angels*

In 1981, Steve Mariotti was mugged by five teenagers. Reflecting afterwards that they looked as though they came from disadvantaged communities, he decided to help kids like the ones who attacked him. He decided to teach disadvantaged youths. Even though he held an MBA from the University of Michigan and had worked in the corporate world as a financial analyst and later a small-business owner, he took a teaching position in special education at a high school in the Morrisania section of the Bronx.

His mission of helping grew stronger as he noticed that the most resistant youths in his class, the young men, grew interested in their schoolwork when he spoke about the basics of starting their own business. With this insight, he acquired a $20,000 grant from the Boys and Girls Clubs of Newark and launched the National Foundation for Teaching Entrepreneurship (NFTE) in 1987. His goal was to improve society by teaching young people to start and operate their own small businesses.

According to a 1994 Gallup survey, 69 percent of high school students are interested in starting a business. Steve's firsthand experience confirms this data. To date, NFTE has helped more than eighteen thousand young people start businesses. The program is currently offered in fourteen cities in the United States. According to Bobby Austin, program officer

---

of the W. K. Kellogg Foundation, extensive research shows the NFTE program to be a national leader in the field of youth entrepreneurship education.

As Steve says, "What other NFTE teachers and I have observed is that our students are less likely to have unwanted pregnancies and more likely to graduate from high school, develop self-esteem, and go to college. There is something about learning to start and operate one's own small business that is very inspiring for these young people."

Through the NFTE program—which includes entrepreneurial basics such as cost-benefit analysis, record keeping, advertising, and marketing—teens get the help they need to grow successful small businesses. "Teaching entrepreneurship is the single most important thing we can do to improve the lives of the poor," he says. As one young graduate of NFTE states, "My dream is not to die in poverty but to have poverty die in me."

Steve's passion to bring a new vision to troubled children in inner cities drives his daily work. When asked what makes a graduate successful, he quickly replies, "NFTE is just a tiny part compared to our students' spirituality, personal discipline, love, courage, and hope." He also sees all seven of the "angel beliefs" that this book discusses as important to his life's work, which is to create value in the marketplace by providing economic literacy for every child. "Thirteen million children live in poverty," he says. "If they learn the principles of wealth creation and ownership just as they learn their multiplication tables, we would find a world filled with more creative, passionate, and purposeful people." Right now there are only ten thousand kids graduating yearly in economic literacy programs like the one his organization runs. Together with partnerships with such corporations as Microsoft, NFTE can now implement creative processes that include replicating its program on the Internet. This allows schools to access a significant part of the program at a much lower cost.

Within a handful of years, Steve's program has opened the door for many miracles, such as the one that Michelle Lee Araujo experienced.

Michelle grew up in extremely poor conditions. In and out of foster homes for many years, she eventually ended up a mother of three at the age of nineteen, while living on welfare in the South End of New Bedford, Massachusetts.

But in 1991, Michelle's life changed. Through an opportunity to enroll in NFTE, she turned her life around. She had a business idea: to travel to New York to buy clothes at wholesale prices and sell them at retail back in New Bedford. Because she had no overhead in selling the clothes out of her home, she could offer prices lower than retail stores did. She had in mind a method of selling clothes that was destined to be a strong success: through organized parties.

Today, Michelle is a senior at the University of Massachusetts-Dartmouth and a dean's list student. She has been a guest speaker at programs for teenage mothers, sharing her story and encouraging them to take up entrepreneurism as a ticket out of poverty. This is just the kind of result Steve was hoping for when he started NFTE.

Steve Mariotti is an excellent example of the many wonderful people who embody the beliefs of workplace angels. Seven beliefs illustrate the power wielded by workplace angels, as seen in how each one applies to Steve himself:

1. *Faith.* Steve has faith that the program will continue to serve teens in need; likewise, although there have been difficult times he has tapped into faith to find the strength to keep his vision alive.

2. *Hope.* He brings hope to these children every day. In turn, the kids have hope they can pull themselves out of poverty, both psychologically and financially.

3. *Charity.* As is typical of many workplace angels, he downplays his belief in charity by saying he enjoys his work so much and is serving his self-interest through NFTE. But his charitable impulse is clear as he explains: "If I were a billionaire, I would do this work anyway. The satisfaction I receive is tremendous. There is a career path here for many others like me—just an average person who wants to make a difference in the lives of others. Almost every day, it is pure joy. There are tragic situations, as when a child is killed, and I suffer greatly from them. I get twenty calls a day from graduates in leadership positions in nonprofits. This is truly a great career path that I believe more people should explore."

4. *Courage.* Steve needed courage to enter the New York school system in the 1980s, when the establishment was very resistant to teaching lower-income individuals entrepreneurism. He then kept his courage throughout the next seven years, until he found a school that would support his program.

5. *Truth.* NFTE teachers are genuine with their students. Steve comments: "Truth is the hallmark of any good teacher—straight talk with the kids, so long as they don't feel as though they are being put down. One kid is arrogant; another has a personal hygiene problem; another is always late. To share with each one the truth with a loving attitude is our goal."

6. *Trust.* Steve's program shows students how to build trust in one another. In Steve's words, "I always try to do exactly what I say. Through truth I build trust." Believing that building trust requires active involvement in teaching and mentoring, he spends about twenty hours a week teaching and meeting with parents, kids, and teachers.

7. *Love.* "Love means achieving," Steve emphasizes. "You've got to love. That should be repeated every workday to every person—even those toward whom you may have great anger."

Like the other workplace angels showcased throughout this book, Steve Mariotti shows that your work and the value you get out of it are strongly linked to your commitment to serving others.

This book is for people who want to recreate their workspaces. Notice I do not say "workplaces." Your workspace is the area you work in daily. Within that small environment, you can create a better place for all—if you *choose* to. As your workspace changes, your world of work starts to reflect your efforts. By making a positive difference in the lives of others, you make your work more satisfying. Through these angel stories and strategies, you find the elusive workplace in which you have always wanted to work.

This book is also for managers who are looking for tools to transform the workplace—but change it from the heart, which is where real change happens. As one division head said to me, "I work on all the change initiatives upper management pushes, allowing my employees to come up with the answers themselves. I don't tell them what they should do. Rather, I *ask* them, and believe it or not, they come to the same solutions—with ownership of the problem, to boot!"

There is universal cynicism in the workplace. People want change. They want to do things differently because what they are currently doing is not working. Younger people are jaded; they see allegiance to a company doesn't pay off the way it used to. Middle-aged, middle managers might have been skeptical before, but in many cases they are now outwardly bitter. Even those who are somewhere in the executive tier of organizations are shifting their interests to other pursuits besides corporate ladder climbing.

The truth of the desire for change is not just in the corporate world. Doctors are worried about the shrinking revenues of health provider organizations as Medicare and Medicaid eat away at earnings. Lawyers, accountants, and consultants, too, grow cynical as they put in their time only to find that they are competing harder for partnerships that may not be there when these professionals are due for such rewards for their work. Meanwhile, millions of small-business owners struggle to keep their enterprises afloat.

The world really is changing. There will never be the security there once was. Old beliefs don't work anymore. We need something to sustain ourselves. Ask yourself how you are going to create meaningful space in your life. You face counterproductive actions taking place in the workplace every day. For example, do you work in a company whose diversity initiative is really working? If you answer no, you are not alone. So many organizations are using the jargon of positive change but not "walking the talk." Employees have come to expect less and less, but isn't there some breaking point? How many times do employees attend motivational sessions, inside or outside the office, only to return to a reality quite different from the encouraging one of the session? How long before the company is willing to make a strong commitment?

Toward a New Tomorrow

The culture (that is, atmosphere, spirit) of an organization is influenced in more ways than any of us can conceive by the attitudes of its members.

—CAROLYN WARNER, POLITICAL LEADER

What is your attitude toward work today? Are you satisfied? Do you think your coworkers are satisfied? What can be done to improve your workplace? What if you begin taking those actions today? Do you think that your attitude would improve if everyone in your organization cared more about each other? Believe it or not, I have interviewed hundreds of people who, tired of waiting for a change from on high, decided to take matters into their own hands. They started performing small acts of caring that have added value to their workplaces. These people now see things differently. They realize they can take action and improve the conditions of their work environment.

As one workplace angel states: "There is a paradox in America. With all its abundance . . . we are so lacking. We probably give, as a culture and more than any other culture, our time and money. On the other hand, as a capitalist society we have more greed than any other country. On top of this, we have a free press so we can talk more about this overriding flaw. It isn't surprising, therefore, that so many of our young people make choices that tend to focus on their own self-gain."

In writing this book, I want to offer you the reader an opportunity to think differently about what it means to add value at work, while at the same time adding value to your own life so that you enter and exit your workplace spiritually empowered. Wherever you work, constantly feeding your own spirit and the spirit of those with whom you come in daily contact is essential. Without constant soul nurturing, we become empty, shallow, and joyless.

Having served as a speaker at retreats on spirituality in the workplace, I have come to see the great importance of soul nurturing. I have encountered people from all walks of life in those retreats, from judges to janitors, teachers to truck drivers, nurses to nannies. The group discussions unleashed great passion about issues of workplace spirituality. I never knew when someone would suddenly decide to share a soul-nurturing story about bringing spiritual beliefs into the workplace. I would be awestruck, listening to stories of people acting like angels in emergency rooms, on truck routes, in classrooms, and in corporate corridors. Each person who spoke made it clear, however, that he or she was constantly challenged personally as to how to take—and then, more important, sustain—their Sunday morning spirituality in their Monday morning workplaces.

Year after year, I returned to the retreats to share my challenges, walking my spiritual talk in my own workplace. Each time I would leave determined to do a better job the following year. We all knew it was not easy to espouse spiritual beliefs in the world of work. As M. Scott Peck says profoundly in the three opening words of his landmark book, *The Road Less Traveled,* "Life is difficult." He must have had in mind the challenge of bringing spirituality into the workplace when he wrote that revealing statement!

I reflected on my life. Just past the age of forty, I was still struggling to see how to bring my strong values and beliefs into the many places I worked as a speaker, consultant, and trainer. I went back over my journals, and even my childhood diaries, for the past thirty years. I looked for patterns of beliefs I had developed throughout my life that influenced the choices I made and actions I took in various workplaces, as well as at home with my husband and two children. I included my home life in the search because I realized that what we take into the workplace truly begins at home.

What I found were the seven beliefs, or values, I have already listed. They had become an integrated part of how I would make choices and what actions I would take as a result of those choices. As I started to research these beliefs, I found that each one was a strong catalyst in how I live my life today, every day. Through this realization, I found I was experiencing even more profound positive change in my life because of my heightened awareness of these beliefs. I found I was more *on purpose* and therefore spoke and acted with more clarity, authority, and power. One of my long-term clients, with whom I have shared this process, recently said, "Now that I know what my beliefs and values are, I can't imagine telling someone *what* I do at work without first sharing my beliefs. They tell others *who* I am."

I started observing how other people act based on one or more of these seven beliefs and discovered how valuable they are for those who act on them daily. Working through my large network, I asked everyone if they held any of these seven beliefs, and if so, how they had conducted their lives on that basis. I soon became swamped with calls from people referring their favorite workplace angels (the term I use for people who embody these beliefs in the world of work). I have put as many of these people in this book as I possibly could. It is an inspiration to know that there are many more powerful workplace angels than I ever thought imaginable.

Seven Traits of the Old and New Worlds of Work

Following is a list of the current beliefs so often held in the workplace, juxtaposed with those beliefs emerging from the efforts of leaders—the workplace angels.

How It Is	*How It Can Be*
Doubt	Faith
Pessimism	Hope
Selfishness	Charity
Fear	Courage
White lies (excused as politics or outright dishonesty)	Truth
Disbelief	Trust
Hate (or anger)	Love

What Is in This Book and How to Use It

E ach of the seven beliefs of powerful workplace angels has
   its own chapter. Additionally, I wish to show how the beliefs work well in tandem with one another. You may recognize that in some chapters other beliefs are intertwined. This
is not to confuse you but to help you use the beliefs as a *system*
for positive change in your workplace.

Each chapter begins with an overview of the angel belief, sharing insights as to the origins and use of each belief
throughout the ages. The chapter then showcases a number of
workplace angels, people who embody that belief every day.
Through the stories, we hear the words and share the experience of the world of work that each angel has cocreated in his
or her workplace.

Located at the end of each chapter is a section with strategic questions for reflection, along with action steps to help you
create a workplace filled with angels. You can act on your own
or create a team of angels to change how you work. The chapter then offers an Angel Advice Corner, suggesting even more
ways to bring that belief into your work. Finally, each chapter
has a summary of the angel actions already listed in the chapter along with the reflections; the Angel Action Summary is
meant to be photocopied and put up for daily inspiration and
direction.

I hope that this book brings you new commitment and
passion to your work life and your home life. It surprises me
to see how often I now acknowledge one of my teenage sons,
or my husband, or a friend for actively showing one of the
seven angel beliefs in their lives. In fact, I find I have created
a whole new vocabulary—and a powerful one—for praising
and appreciating others.

My wish for you echoes the words of one of my favorite
poets, Robert Louis Stevenson: "To be what we are and to be-

come what we are capable of becoming, is the only end in life." Serving others is our best strategy for becoming all that we can be; may this book open the door to endless possibilities for you!

A Final Note Before You Begin

This is not a Pollyanna book. It is filled with hundreds of anecdotes and stories of real people who hold and put into practice one or more of the beliefs of workplace angels. These people are more satisfied with their work and more productive; as a result, they make their organizations more profitable. Although there might not currently be extensive scientific studies to support the belief that ethical behavior leads to higher profitability, it is certain that there is an incredible surge in our need to make work more meaningful. Angels in workplaces are everywhere; almost everyone has their own story to tell. Come with me into the lives of the many angels showcased in this book, and experience a new world of work—a world where what you believe is just as important as what you do.

FAITH

*Believing in "What Is"
and "What Could Be"*

*Faith without works is like a bird without wings; though she
may hop about on earth, she will never fly to heaven. But
when both are joined together, then doth the soul mount up
to her eternal rest.*

—Francis Beaumont

The word *faith* comes from the Latin *fidere*, which means "to trust." Further definitions add that faith is a belief resting in the divine rather than the logical. In the New Testament, faith is "the substance of things hoped for, the evidence of things not seen." All of these definitions build a connection between what starts in our heads and is then continuously supported in our hearts. Angels in the workplace carry the belief of faith, using both their heads and hearts to lead them through daily challenges.

Faith is not necessarily founded in the divine, but without reference to divinity the force of the word is dramatically diminished. For example, you can have faith that the project you are currently working on will be successful, by which you mean that you trust you did your best and therefore will be rewarded for your efforts. Yet those who embrace faith in a divinity further hold a deep conviction that the best possible outcome will result, even though it might not be seen by others as positive. Those with a divine faith believe that their spiritual needs are always being served and that material outcomes finish a distant second to the needs of the soul. In the example of the successful project, the person with a spiritual faith is satisfied regardless of the material outcome. The goal is always to serve; if the goal has been met, then soul needs are met.

Do you have faith in your workplace? If your answer is a resounding "No!" then you are certainly not alone. There are millions like you who feel disconnected and vulnerable to workplace challenges, from increased responsibilities to decreased pay and job loss. The workplace angels showcased in this chapter have used the belief of faith as a tool for creating a new world of work. They have realized success by living for each other. They carry faith into their workplaces and spread it among their coworkers as a gardener plants precious seeds in a fallow garden bed, empowering others through those deeds.

But you cannot empower people if they choose not to be empowered. The good news is that most people want you to care about them; caring is the first connection necessary to build an empowered workforce. The trick is to do so consciously and consistently. Workplace angels of faith know this.

Angels who embody the belief of faith value the opinions of others in their work environments. They have faith that at every level of an organization there exist people who have valuable knowledge to share. Accordingly, workplace angels use their abilities to nurture the talents of others, adding value to each life they touch.

Angels who embody faith are proactive, sharing their faith in their fellow workers, superiors, suppliers, and customers. They are the ultimate manifesters of the corporate mission because they know what it means to "hold their faith" in what could be. In fact, a recent Gallup poll of fifty-five thousand workers shows that one of the correlations between satisfied workers and improved employee performance is that employees make a mental and emotional link between their work and their company's mission as espoused through the corporate mission statement.

Those employees who share the belief in faith are able to ride out the storms that come from time to time in most workplaces. In turn, they are recognized as role models, showing others through their actions how to handle these downturns. For every dark work day of the soul faced by those in the world of work, workplace angels of faith teach us to believe in better days by carrying our own light of faith, filled with confidence that all will be well.

The Purest Act of Faith

That woman made a difference in my life! I can't wait to get out every day and sell papers.

DAN GILROY, *WORKPLACE ANGEL*

The Alpha Project, a program for homeless men, puts them in jobs in the local community of Vista, California. One of the jobs the men take on is selling newspapers on busy street corners. Clad in bright red and yellow vests, these men are taught to sell daily papers with a smile, a wave, and a nice word for everyone. I had the pleasure of meeting some of the graduates of the program during a community conference I facilitated, where we honored the town's top three community initiatives. Every graduate with whom I spoke (there were about twenty) shared his deep commitment to serving Alpha colleagues and helping new graduates go through their very intense and difficult rehabilitation program.

One man, Dan Gilroy, came up to me during the conference and told me about an experience he had while selling newspapers one day. Dan said a woman pulled over in her station wagon, jumped out, ran up to him, and hugged him. After he got over his shock, he asked her what was going on. She said,

"I've been driving by your stop for more than three months now. Each day you're out here, rain or shine, waving to people, smiling, and patiently waiting for someone to buy a paper."

Dan went on to say he asked her why his behavior mattered so much to her. She responded, "I lost my son three months ago. When it happened, I didn't want to live. Each day I drove by you, I thought it would be my last. I wanted to commit suicide. Yet each day you would wave at me and I would put it off for another day. Soon I started looking forward to you being here. I started to think more about you and how you show up with what looks like daily renewed faith even though you don't know what tomorrow might bring. I started thinking that if you could stay alive and give to the world, even though you were hurting, so could I!"

This homeless man looked at me with the greatest glow of joy in his eyes and said, "You know, Melissa, that woman made a difference in my life! I can't wait to get out every day and sell papers." Needless to say, I was thoroughly humbled by that man and every one of them in the Alpha project. They understand what faith means in the workspace and how important it is.

Since that time, Dan has found full-time employment. He now has his own apartment. As Chris Megison, regional director of the Alpha Project, stated, "What stands out with Dan is his constant commitment to the Alpha Project. He was dubbed our community chaplain because he always had some spiritual message to share. He would quote something biblical or from a famous person during our meetings. He still comes back every two weeks when we get in a new group of men. He is constantly passing on his wisdom: how he developed the faith to get off the streets and how he now has faith that this group will accomplish similar goals to his. Dan is a great communicator, very simple and down-to-earth; he has done as much for others as for himself. That is rather unusual in someone with his background: his dedication to give back so quickly. He is so open and honest—it rubs off on the other men!"

Maybe it is easier for these men to have faith, some may say, since after all they have no place to go but up. What I learned from spending time with these powerful workplace angels is that each one must move from that horrible abyss called hopelessness into a pure state of faith: that tomorrow will not be just like today, that they can have a better life than the one they have been leading, that there is a future for them where they will be accepted as people who have something to share with society.

———— ANGEL REFLECTIONS AND ACTIONS ————

Reflection What small amount of faith can you hold in your heart today that will help you make your workplace just a little brighter?

Reflection How can you share your faith in others in your workplace today?

Reflection How can you use your smile as a tool to promote joy in your workplace?

Action Find those colleagues, customers, and suppliers—those kindred spirits—with whom you can share your belief in faith. Expecting nothing in return, let them know how much you appreciate them. For example, I make annual phone calls around Thanksgiving to tell others how thankful I am they are in my life.

Through Their Faith They Brought Down a Giant

Faith is to believe what we do not see; and the reward of this faith is to see what we believe.

—St. Augustine

Bring together a legal secretary, a housewife, a photocopy repairman, a bond trader, a computer analyst, and a garbage truck driver, and what do you get? If you are talking about the residents of West Chicago, you have "the Thorium Group"—an army of angels.

Cindy Pepple was the bond trader of the group. Along with just a handful of ordinary citizens, she brought down an energy and chemical company in a landmark case that cost the giant millions before it was over. One of the chemicals that the company produced was thorium, which is used to make the ever-burning mantels in lanterns. The company buried this very toxic waste in poorly sealed containers throughout the 1960s, until its factory in West Chicago closed.

It was more than two decades later, after a number of residents developed cancer, that the townspeople of West Chicago started investigating the possibility that these people were dying from other than "natural causes."

Throughout the fight against the chemical company, the small band of residents never lost faith that they would be able to create change (as well as finding safety in numbers). They used their job skills along the way to expedite their efforts. For example, the photocopier repairman used his service calls as opportunities to make copies of petitions. Every time he tested a copier after repair, he used one of the group's petition forms as the master in running off a hundred or so test-run copies. Pepple, who understood stockholder statements, was able to teach other members of the group how to read them and use their understanding at a shareholder meeting.

The Thorium Group also employed some clever tactics to make its point. They used permanent markers to write on the bottom of several hundred yellow plastic ducks, "If you're getting this duck, this is not all you're getting." The ducks made major news when they were set afloat from West Chicago down the Fox River, which flowed through a number of other towns. The stunt showed that thorium poorly contained in area landfills had a good chance of getting into the water and traveling to other cities, with similar results in the incidence of cancer. When the group realized that the ducks themselves were not environmentally friendly, they recovered them and, rather than throw them away, had a number of them bronzed.

They then glued each duck to a base with an engraved plaque. These "awards" were given to the state legislators who helped pass a law banning thorium dumping (as well as fining the chemical company for each year it stalled performing a proper cleanup). The plaque read, "Thanks for not ducking out on us!"

With this creative mix of humor and strategy, the members of the Thorium Group maintained their faith that they could make a difference in their community. Today most of the group members—people who had never before thought of this kind of giving back—are involved in some form of community work in their town. They have become beacons of faith shining their power to make a difference throughout the reaches of the community.

——————— ANGEL REFLECTIONS AND ACTIONS ———————

Reflection How can you get involved in a project in your community where you can share your faith in creating a better place for all?

Reflection What vision do you have for your community?

Action Start a small project with just a couple of friends or neighbors. One small group of teachers turned a nuisance into a learning site. Tired of worrying whether a young child might fall into a standing pool of water near the school playground, they inspired people to donate they labor and money needed to fill it in and build a "prairie garden." The site became a place where children could learn about the plants and flowers growing in their own special community.

A Woman of Great Faith

My faith and belief in this project to empower children made it succeed.

MOMMA HAWK, WORKPLACE ANGEL

Recovering the Gifted Child is a school program like no other in the city of Chicago—probably like none in the United States. It is obvious why: there is no other woman like Momma

Hawk. Recovering the Gifted Child is the brainchild of Momma Hawk (born Corla Powell), a public school teacher for whom the schoolhouse is the workplace.

Frustrated with seeing student after student fall through the cracks academically, Momma Hawk pulled together $1,500 of her own money and began a quest to educate children her own way. She approached her principal with her idea and was allowed to occupy a wing of the school for her "academy."

To attend, students (and their parents) have to sign a contract agreeing to remain under Momma Hawk's guidance until they graduate. To some, this may sound extreme. But with more than 350 kids on the program waiting list, she seems to be doing something right! All but two of the sixty-five students who have attended the Recovering the Gifted Child Academy's four-year program have gone on to finish high school. You have to ask yourself, How does she do it? How do you keep these kids motivated, when immediately outside the school doors is the neighborhood with more homicides than any other Chicago school district?

In a tough curriculum, each student takes such fundamentals as reading, writing, and math along with programs the likes of City Planning Design (which is taught in science). Civic lessons are taught through a program called Communicating with Congress. Life skills are equally important at RGCA, as students learn subject areas such as entrepreneurship. Here, time is devoted to learning how to own and operate a store, market a product, and balance accounts. Students actually run clothing and craft shops open to the public at the school's minimall.

All of these opportunities, however, would not be possible if not for the absolute faith of Momma Hawk, who reflects that "My faith and belief in this project to empower children made it succeed." She kept that faith knowing she could help children no matter what obstacles arose.

Born in Chicago, Corla Powell grew up in a family of eight children. She says she was the rule breaker of the group. Although an excellent student (she went on to earn a bachelor of science degree in business education), she simply had a difficult time with authority. Luckily, a neighbor, Joyce Batson, was one of her teachers; Joyce recognized something special in Corla and began mentoring her, helping to instill confidence and "dethroning her bully act." At twenty-five, Corla realized her dream to become a teacher. The rest, as they say, is history.

Her personal struggles were enough to challenge the strongest of souls. At twenty-eight, she survived uterine cancer. Four years later, doctors removed a malignant tumor from her breast. That same year, her marriage ended. Corla attempted suicide by overdosing on antidepressants prescribed by her doctor. It was during these overwhelming trials, she says, that "God gave me a dream to take care of children who had been rejected. I literally saw myself going around the world hugging and loving children nobody else wanted." She says she does not get discouraged. She just keeps on "pushin' and keepin' the faith." Hundreds of children and parents are grateful today for that degree of faith.

——————— ANGEL REFLECTIONS AND ACTIONS ———————

Reflection What experiences have you had that tested your faith?

Action Donate your time to help a rejected child reconnect with the world. There are so many organizations that offer this opportunity: mentoring programs, Big Brothers and Big Sisters, the Girl Scouts, and others (see the Resource section in the back for more direction).

Out of the Darkness of Doubt, into the Light of Faith

I gave a presentation a few years ago at a law firm handling insurance litigation. The audience was predominantly women legal secretaries. I was asked to present on customer service during a ninety-minute lunch break. The participants were to come into the room and pick up their box lunches; once they were seated, I was to begin the presentation. I understood that the firm thought it was really doing the secretaries a favor by giving them an extra half hour!

The atmosphere was so tense and negative that day, I remember praying that I would be able to impart any words of wisdom or even comfort that could make a difference for these women. Even as they filed past me to get their box lunches, they were grumbling to one another or staring fixedly at the ground, not wanting to make any conversation. I thought, if it had not been for the person who brought me in (who was much more positive than the attendees), I would never have taken the assignment. No one likes to be put in a no-win position. But here I was, and the training had to go on.

Throughout the presentation, I noticed only one or two women showing interest in what I was saying. I could tell the rest thought otherwise. When I opened up the discussion on improving customer service, I immediately heard a startling comment: "How can we even think about doing anything for others when we can't even go to the bathroom during the day?"

All I could say was, "What do you mean?"

"We are so tied to our bosses' billable hours that we often don't take lunch breaks or go to the bathroom all day."

I was shocked. (But not long afterwards, I found out that in a number of organizations this is true for many women.) I began talking to these legal secretaries about what they could do for each other to make their work load easier—so that at the least they could take care of some of their basic needs.

At first there was no response. These employees were so used to thinking in survival mode they had difficulty seeing how they could move past that mind-set. I waited for an uncomfortable minute and was finally about to offer some suggestions when one secretary stood up and said, "I could come around to a couple of women's desks daily and make sure they take a break. I have a bit more free time right now because my attorney is working on a big trial."

Slowly, more of them came up with ideas on how they could help one another. One would buy lunch for a week for two other secretaries and herself. They could take turns making photocopies for one another. They could designate a special week for each employee in a group of four to go out after work, so that the other three could buy for the fourth. They could have early breakfasts, to exchange inspirational stories and energize one another for the workday. Soon clusters of groups came together in the room to make commitments to each other.

I spoke about their having faith that they could make a difference for one another. Faith that they were closer to one another's needs and together could make life easier for all. Faith that they could hold on to for one another.

Of course, one or two people came up to me afterward to say, "Things aren't going to change here. They've always been the same!" But some walked out of the room determined to create positive change. Those who left with that attitude have indeed made continuous improvements since that day; I know this because I have gone back to the same firm several times, and each time the group is more prepared to take on the actions of powerful workplace angels (except for a few who still want to hold on to their attitude of it's-never-going-to-change). The majority still have faith that sooner or later these few will also come around. Through the faith of the inspired secretaries, a number of the others have chosen to shift their paradigm of the painful workplace, seeing how they can participate in a renaissance of the spirit.

As one employee shared with me, "Our increased productivity and a decrease in the number of errors in our documents has generated better pay and more free time for those of us who held our faith—not in what is but in what could be at our firm. It's a funny thing about faith. Those who believed reaped the rewards of their beliefs, while those who chose to operate as usual are still back where they were three months ago!"

——————— ANGEL REFLECTIONS AND ACTIONS ———————

Reflection　What beliefs sustain you and give you faith during difficult times?

Action　Champion a session in your workplace to share ideas for developing faith, as the group did in this story. Ask your colleagues what they can do for themselves and each other that brings their belief in faith to their lives at work.

Faith Above All Else

By keeping our faith and a sense of humor, we can reclaim our power to take control of our lives.

DAVE CAREY, WORKPLACE ANGEL

Dave Carey spent twenty-six years in the U.S. Navy as a pilot. He was shot down in Vietnam and spent five long years as a prisoner of war. The experience led Dave to tap into his belief in faith that he would return home safely. Today he uses this defining story to tell others to have faith that they are powerful, resourceful, resilient beings. He spends about half his time speaking and the other half as a trainer.

One of the things Dave speaks of often is his faith in God. For him, having faith creates the courage to move through even the worst tragedies in life: "One of the things I see in the workplace is an enormous number of people doing things they don't like to do—that they aren't passionate about. They feel like they are trapped, that they have no alternatives. They are unhappy for a lot of reasons—not so much that they are not in good jobs, but that these jobs are not bringing them joy. They keep themselves in these positions because they think they are powerless to change." Dave helps people tap into their own dormant power by first helping them recognize it exists and can be reclaimed at any moment.

Dave comments that "by keeping our faith and a sense of humor, we can reclaim our power to take control of our lives." His prescription is to

- Do your best.
- Do what you have to do.
- Keep your sense of humor.
- Choose to grow.
- Keep the faith—faith in yourself, faith in each other, faith in your country, faith in God.

Following a morning speech at a large corporation, a huge Texan came up to Dave and asked, "May I talk to you?" Dave said sure, and with that the man threw his arm around him and steered him down the hall. He said, "In this lifetime, we are all going to get shot down—some of us more than once." With that, the Texan proceeded to tell him about how his eighteen-year-old son had died recently. The man talked about picking up the pieces for the six months since his son's death. He then went down Dave's prescription list, affirming how important the ideas were in helping anyone struggling through difficult times.

When Dave's wife died of breast cancer in 1997, he had to tap into his faith to get through the ordeal—the same belief in faith he had developed in Vietnam. Many people come up to him after his talks to say, "That's just what I needed to hear." These are gifts of thanks to Dave, who prays for his audiences and his clients. He puts it simply: "We all need prayers."

—————— ANGEL REFLECTIONS AND ACTIONS ——————

Reflection What things are you worrying about the most? What prayers can you say that would help you surrender those worries to a higher power?

Action Find someone in or outside the workplace who espouses belief in faith. Talk to the person. Ask for his story as to how he developed that belief. Ask for his support in helping you build your belief in faith in your workplace.

Faith and Contagious Enthusiasm

It is miraculous to see people change when they see they have choices. They open up like roses if they see they can make a difference—that they do have value. It is so joyful to watch them unfold.

BARBARA GLANZ, WORKPLACE ANGEL

Barbara Glanz clearly models the belief in faith in the workplace. Today, she is a renowned professional speaker, trainer, and author who has spoken on three continents and in forty-six states. She says, "Because of my faith in the Lord and his direction in my life, I was able to move out of a very good corporate position at a tough time in my life." In 1994, her husband was getting ready to retire after thirty years with the *Chicago Tribune*, they had two children in college, and she had a great job as an executive with Kaset, a Times-Mirror training company. It was a big risk to go out on her own.

However, Barbara's faith in God's direction in her life and her sense of mission in the work she was doing gave her the courage she needed. Her gift of being able to touch people's hearts, inspire them, get their creative juices going, and prompt them individually to make a difference for themselves and others in their workplaces has built for her a lucrative business.

Barbara's faith in God—and resultant faith in herself and
her abilities, even when it is not expressed overtly—gives other
people faith in their *own* abilities and a deep sense of purpose.
They are in turn led to productive action. People hearing her
speeches, reading her books, and attending her seminars talk
about her power to create what she calls "contagious enthusiasm." One seminar attendee eloquently shares this experience:
"I had just had the absolute worst day and dealt with what
seemed at the time the worst people. Very downhearted, I
went to the seminar. The last thing on my mind was worrying
about my customer's needs—what about me?! Why should I
be nice to everyone else? Thank you for caring, Barbara; you
knocked my socks off and brought tears to my eyes twice and
have renewed my spirit. I'm walking away much better and
happier than when I came in."

A fan letter shares some of Barbara's techniques for regenerating spirit: "For me, this training session is more than
learning to interact better with the public. It's about you and
me and each person in the world. It reminds me of our creativity, gentleness, and intelligence as human beings. It reminds me that we are all different but can still sit in harmony
at the same table."

With results like these, it is clear that Barbara is offering
something *beyond* words; she is extending an offer to others to
share her faith. She attributes her work success to the fact that
people are so overwhelmed with change and technology that
they think they have no choices. She adds, "It is miraculous to
see people change when they see they have choices. They
open up like roses if they see they can make a difference—that
they do have value. It is joyful to watch them unfold."

Through her inspiring stories, she shares how faith helped
her through some of life's harshest challenges, including the loss
of a child. She offers her stories to help others ease their personal struggles. In one story, a little girl was savagely attacked

by a dog; her scalp was almost torn away. Today she is a woman of faith, who remembers from that incident only the very loving doctors and nurses embracing her gently as they placed hundreds of stitches in her scalp with no anesthesia. She grew up to become the powerful workplace angel of faith, Barbara Glanz.

Her faith is both spiritual and practical. Offering her audiences dozens of inspirational stories, she calls on them to have faith even when there seems little hope. She is a workplace angel, showing us all that we can share our faith not in what is but in what could be, with our colleagues at work.

—————— ANGEL REFLECTIONS AND ACTIONS ——————

Reflection Who is in need of your support, your faith in what could be, today?

Reflection What belief do you have in faith?

Action Through kind words or prayer, remember those in your workplace who are in need. I regularly pray for those who confide that they are in difficult circumstances. Whatever your beliefs, kind thoughts or prayer can make a world of difference.

Angel Advice Corner

Bringing More Faith into Your Workplace

Here are some simple tips for bringing more faith into your workplace. Review them regularly for further direction in building the power of faith in your world of work.

- *Who in your circle of friends and colleagues needs your faith today?* Pick one person and focus on her needs just for the day. Pray for her. She does not even have to know it. The power of God works in her life just the same.

- *What one thing can you do to make a difference in someone's world?* Share a good book, quote, or poem? An angel in the workplace at the corporate offices of a supermarket chain, Mary Woods, sends e-mail with inspirational quotes to her fellow coworkers every day. She finds that if she does not get the quote out by 10:00 A.M., her colleagues come looking for her, requesting "their" quote.

- *Do what it takes to make your workplace better for yourself and others.* All the angels I have spoken to about faith agree that it relates to your ability to be on God's time clock, not your own. Most of the time, this means sticking to your plan to make things better, while understanding that you do not control how your actions actually bring about the positive change you so deeply want (and many times need). This is not to say that you do not have choices; you can always change jobs or positions. Only you know what is right for you; it comes from taking time every day to be quiet, to ask yourself the question in this reflection and listen for the answer.

- *Replace old beliefs with better, more productive ones.* A negative thought keeps presenting itself to you until you replace it with an equally powerful and opposing good thought.

My Past Beliefs

I can't change anything.

It's too hard.

My New Beliefs

I have faith that I can make a difference.

I give myself permission to serve.

- *Pray for those you would not otherwise think of praying for.* Managers at a collection agency came up with the idea of a faith exercise: praying for their debtors that they might find the funds to pay off their debts as soon as possible. The organization has let the creditors who are its primary customers know that staff are praying for the debtors. Managers have been pleased by both the positive support for their actions and the results. The collection agency continues to experience rapid growth and great profitability. But the best part, the owner says, is that her employees have been much easier to work with now that they feel less stress in a job that is usually rather depressing, to say the least!

- *Walk the talk.* Do you have faith, or do you just talk about having faith? The answer to this question is revealed each time you face life's challenges with faith rather than fear.

- *Tap into your faith through your heart, not your head.* Faith is felt in the heart, not the head. Developing better sensitivity to what emanates from your heart rather than from your head takes time (and faith!). Spend five minutes a day just focusing your thoughts on your heart. At the end of this time, think about the things that are troubling you at the moment. Feel the power emanating from your heart. As you spend time practicing this tapping into the power of faith through you heart, you will grow more aware of your ability to navigate life's frequently rough waters.

- *Use this prayer:* Dear God, give me the faith I need to go into the workplace today and serve my customers, coworkers, suppliers, and superiors.

Faith: A Summary of Angel Actions

Find those colleagues, customers, and suppliers—kindred spirits—with whom you can share your belief in faith. Expecting nothing in return, let them know how much you appreciate them.

Start a small project with just a couple of friends or neighbors. (Recall the example of a small group of teachers who solicited donations of labor and money to turn the nuisance of a standing pool of water near the school playground into a learning site, a "prairie garden.")

Donate your time to help a rejected child reconnect with the world. There are so many organizations that offer this opportunity: mentoring programs, Big Brothers and Big Sisters, the Girl Scouts, and others.

Champion a session in your workplace to share ideas for developing faith, as did the group of legal secretaries in this chapter. Ask your colleagues what they can do for themselves and each other that brings their belief in faith to their lives at work.

Find someone in or outside the workplace that espouses the belief in faith. Talk to that person. Ask for their story of how they developed that belief. Ask for their support in helping you build your belief of faith in your workplace.

Through kind words or prayer, remember those in your workplace who are in need. Whatever your beliefs, kind thoughts or prayer can make a world of difference.

∞

HOPE

Creating Self-Fulfilling Optimism

It is difficult to say what is impossible for us. The dream of yesterday is the hope of today and the reality of tomorrow.

—Robert Goddard

Hope is just as important as faith. Yet many in our modern world would disagree, saying that hope is a diluted version of faith. In fact, poets throughout history have used the word *hope* to refer to someone who is "weak" or "pitiful." But there are many examples to illustrate the strength and power of this value.

As with faith, at the base of hope is trust. Faith and hope both require trust that no matter what happens, the result is the best possible outcome. Hope also means "to look forward to with confidence and expectation; to expect and desire." This signals confidence that something you desire will in fact become reality. Spiritually, hope plays an important role in our lives. In the Jewish and Christian faiths, it is recognized as a virtue equal to the beliefs of faith and love. By its linguistic connection throughout history to the word *love*, Christian hope also implies unselfishness and desire to receive hope, in turn to share it with others. In the Christian context, faith, hope, and love cannot exist in isolation because all three values blossom whenever any one is embraced. Within the workplace, hope is often the reason we stay in certain workplaces that offer little joy; we have hope that through our efforts and influence we will bring about a better working environment. We hold onto our value of hope, convinced that through this belief we can make a difference and bring about the changes that improve our lives as well as those of our fellow workers.

I have found in hundreds of hours spent with workplace angels that hope is an important belief that is well put to use. Hope has its own special place in our value system. It often is the foundation for faith. For example, because at first we have hope that we will get a good job, hope leads to faith in ourselves and our abilities, which can attract good job opportunities. Conversely, hope stems from strong faith that the people we work with will produce quality work consistently. We develop further hope that they will stay healthy enough or perhaps interested enough to continue working with us. Hope becomes the blanket that surrounds the value of faith.

Hope can also be born out of truth. If workers choose to share a truth with coworkers and colleagues that they are under no obligation to share, by telling the truth they engender trust and hope among their confidants. Ultimately, they bring hope not only to the others but also to the people whom their confidants interact with. The adage that hope springs eternal is appropriate here, with hope weaving itself like a vine throughout a workplace environment in which people feel they can count on one another. The stories that follow offer you insight into this very important value, so that you can learn to use it for yourself and for the benefit of others.

The Hope of a New Life

Hope is a waking dream.

—ARISTOTLE

The Women's Opportunity Fund provides loans and training to extremely poor women in developing countries to start microbusinesses. With a loan as small as eighty dollars, a woman can start a business and earn enough to feed her family, afford needed health care, and send her children to school.

Because the program has been so successful—98 percent of the women repay their loans—the money is continuously recycled. The women participating in the program have found miraculous transformation in their lives. It develops these women's self-esteem and leadership skills, naturally and as no other assistance could. Not only are their own lives improved dramatically but those of their families and communities are as well.

Currently, more than sixteen thousand women in sixteen countries throughout Latin America, Africa, Asia, and Eastern Europe are participating in this life-changing program. Here is a story illustrating the great hope that just one angel in the workplace has brought to others around her.

Angels Are Worldwide: A Story of Hope from El Salvador

SUSY CHESTON

HER NAME IS ROSA, and her mother calls her Chita. She's in her mid-thirties, with almond-colored skin, shiny black hair, and lively dark eyes. She has four children, of whom my favorite is eight-year-old Xiomara, who loves to kiss and hug.

Rosa was displaced from her home in El Salvador by the 1986 earthquake. She's alone in raising and supporting her children, as are three-fourths of the women in her "marginal community." When I met her, she was living in a dirt-floor shack made of rusted scrap metal, cardboard, and plastic; no windows, lots of mosquitoes. The shack was big enough for the two single beds they shared, nothing else. They threw their clothes across twine that hung just below the ceiling. They bathed outside in their underwear, dipping rainwater from a barrel. Another outside barrel served as a wood stove. Because the "community latrines" were unspeakable and far away, Rosa's kids used the bushes or the nearby garbage dump.

Rosa's best friend, Hilaria, lived next door. She'd been deserted by her common-law husband and lost everything in the earthquake. During the war, she broke her ankle while running from a bomb. Alone, unable to work to feed her six children, she made the agonizing decision to give them up. They are now in an orphanage, and in exchange for ensuring they will be fed, clothed, and educated, Hilaria has had to give up all her rights to see them until they are eighteen. Every Sunday, she takes the bus two hours to hear a five-minute report on her children, then two hours back. Hilaria is often in severe pain from internal injuries but has been unable to get health care. Although she, along with Rosa, was supposed to enter a self-help housing project, her health problems made her unable to pay even the basic amount. In despair, she left the community.

Rosa could have become another Hilaria, but something happened to change her life. Just before Christmas, she got a one hundred dollar loan from the Women's Opportunity Fund.

It's hard to imagine the tremendous impact this small amount had on Rosa's life. Although Rosa doesn't have any work skills, she is a natural entrepreneur. She used her loan to invest in her tiny paper bag business. She bought one hundred dollars' worth of brown paper sheets, cooked up some homemade glue over a wood fire, and used her fingers to spread the glue and turn the paper into rough paper bags. She was able to double her product line—and also her income, from two dollars to four dollars a day.

Since she was making more money, Rosa enrolled her children in both sessions of school. She moved into another shack, still a windowless hovel with a dirt floor, but twice as big. She bought the cable she needed to hook up electricity, and she was able to pay fees so she could participate in the self-help housing project in her community.

The housing project was earthquake relief housing from the archdiocese of San Salvador. A community council was elected to keep records of each person's workdays and to collect the small monthly fees that covered bricklaying and materials. This council, unbeknownst to the archdiocese, started falsifying work and payment records. Suddenly the women in Rosa's squatter settlement were accused of being behind on their commitments and were threatened with being kicked out of the project.

Some of the women, like Rosa, had been working three days a week for five years, hauling sand on their heads and leveling earth, alongside men. Two of the women died of hernias in the process. For five years, they had invested every spare minute and every spare cent in the dream that was held out to them of owning a home, a real home with windows, a home with concrete block walls, a cement floor, electricity, running water, and an indoor latrine. Now they were in danger of losing everything.

The women united to become the Committee of Single Women for Dignity and Progress. I helped them prepare a letter alerting the archdiocese to the corruption. I also arranged a meeting with the archdiocesan head of the housing project. But from then on, it was the women themselves who pushed the boundaries of their culture by challenging the corrupt community council that was embezzling funds. With Rosa as the spokesperson, the archdiocese stepped in to clean up the program. Rosa and my other clients had been in danger of losing their housing rights. Instead, a year after entering the program, they celebrated Christmas in their new homes.

The story gets better. Rosa's loan began to benefit others around her as well. First, she brought her mother, Zoila, into her business. Then, when Zoila's neighbors got interested, Rosa took the time to organize her mother and her mother's neighbors into a solidarity group so that they, too, could get loans. Now Rosa serves as honorary president of that group, and those women are investing their own loans in making planters, fattening geese, and selling homemade hair bands. Rosa became so adept at helping other women organize themselves to receive loans and start businesses that she served as an unofficial loan officer. At one point, I counted thirty-two women who had been directly helped in their businesses by Rosa.

My favorite moment of my year and a half in El Salvador was when I was walking down a dirt path and saw an old woman coming toward me. I kept staring at her, but I couldn't recall who she was. Finally, when she got close to me, I realized it was Zoila. I hadn't recognized her because the old, battered, toothless woman I remembered now had a bright white smile. With her business income, Rosa had bought her mother dentures. The transformation was complete. Zoila looked taller, she exuded confidence, and my spine tingled to see her.

It's the dignity, the renewed hope, the developed self-esteem that are the best payoffs. The beauty of Rosa's story to me is that she did it all. Through her hope, she transformed her own life and the lives of those around her. The small loan from the Women's Opportunity Fund was just the tool she needed to grow the seeds of hope into a beautiful harvest of opportunity.

Reprinted with permission from the Women's Opportunity Fund

We have different parents, different bosses, different circumstances in our lives, but we all take the same hopes and dreams into our workplace every day. Understanding our connectedness empowers us to make a difference. Rosa's story shows us that even the littlest hope can be fanned into a great fire of certainty. I have found that people who hold in their hearts hope for themselves *believe* something better is within their reach. Even further, there are those who hold hope for a better world for others not because they want something in return but because they believe we are all in this thing called life together.

To serve is to realize a gain for all, including yourself. Think about your connections to others. If you are at the workplace now, look around. What dreams do you think the person sitting beside you has? What about the hopes of the people around the corner from you, or on the floors above or below? The hopes and dreams of the people in your building are probably very similar to yours: to feel accepted, cared for, recognized, and appreciated. By focusing on how your hopes interconnect theirs, you turn your attention away from what is not working in your life, toward what you can do to help make someone else's life better. Ultimately, you become a catalyst for positive change in your workplace. Reach down and pull up everyone you can, and sooner rather than later you will find someone reaching down to pull you up even further. The process repeats again and again.

─────── ANGEL REFLECTIONS AND ACTIONS ───────

Reflection Is there anything you feel hopeless about?

Reflection How can you renew your hope by renewing someone else's?

Action Give small doses of hope—through continual acts of caring— to others daily. Many donors of the Women's Opportunity Fund have shared with me that through giving they indeed renew their hope. As they make a profound difference for these women who have so little, they receive renewed hope in their own lives. Small things they take for granted, such as running water or a warm, cozy bed, become much-appreciated luxuries. In turn, they realize how important we all are in connecting to one another to offer hope through small, simple, yet effective acts of caring.

Hope in the ER

My parents always told us kids to open our lives and our doors to others in need. This is my way of giving others hope: through the care I give in the ER.

STEVE ROSKAM, *WORKPLACE ANGEL*

Dr. Steve Roskam is an emergency room physician in an inner-city county hospital in Chicago. Although his life resembles what we see in the television show *ER*, the difference is that he does not have the option of stepping off stage. In this real-life daily drama, he has to be equipped with megadoses of hope. His job is also difficult because where he works resources are often limited: sometimes there are not enough beds, access to specialists is limited, and the types of medication the doctors can distribute are restricted. Steve adds, "Some of our patients are street people. Therefore, if they don't get their medicine at the hospital, they won't be able to get it on the outside because they have no money or public aid; other than the county system, there is no other place they can get help."

He chose to work at a public hospital because that is where he believes he can make the greatest difference. He also believes that "this is where I have the opportunity to apply my faith and the hope it produces in ways most of us could not imagine." This statement was never more evident than the day a three-year-old boy, a victim of severe child abuse, was wheeled into the emergency ward. The boy's uncle had called the paramedics when he went to see his nephew and found him lying unconscious on his bed, his body covered with fresh scars from a beating with an electrical cord. But by the time Steve received him, the little boy was dead. Wounds covered more than half the surface of his limbs and torso, painful evidence of repeated beatings and mutilations, everything from broken bones to cigarette burns. It was the worst thing Steve had ever seen.

"Because of repeated trauma to his tiny body, this precious child had lost his life," he says quietly. "On that particular day, the tragedy overwhelmed me. I had to leave the room. I just wept uncontrollably. At that time, my son Jacob was about the same age. I couldn't look down at that little boy without also seeing my own little boy. I couldn't deal with that degree of being emotionally overwhelmed every day. Those people who do don't last long. With my faith, I have the gift to be present yet not emotionally disabled."

Steve models his beliefs through how he behaves with his residents. With his faith, he delivers hope to a workplace that is literally a battleground of pain and suffering. He loves his work and wakes up every morning with renewed spirit. He tries, no matter what, to get his patients to smile. Of course, that is not always possible, but he makes the effort nonetheless.

He also makes sure that before he exits a patient's room, he puts his hand on her shoulder and says, "We're going to take good care of you." He does so because "my parents always told us kids to open our lives and our doors to others in need. This is my way of giving others hope: through the care I give in the ER."

Steve remembers having people in his home all the time, from foreign exchange students to a friend whose parents were moving to Texas in his senior year. This is where he learned that bringing hope to others was so rewarding.

Steve also shares his belief in hope with the sixty residents he teaches annually. He emphasizes: "Always treat every patient as though they were a beloved member of your family. Every patient that comes into our emergency department has a need. Physically, they need to have their pain taken away, but they may also have additional fears attached to that. For example, one young woman came in with chest pains. Her fear was that as her mother was recently diagnosed with lung cancer she might now have it too. My job was to treat both her emotional and physical pain." The woman walked away from the ER that day with a renewed belief in hope.

With limited resources, days jam-packed with stress, and constant unexpected tragedies, Steve embodies the calm force of hope. Through his constant connection to his faith, he is the rare combination of a man of hope and a strong champion of the needy.

────────── ANGEL REFLECTIONS AND ACTION ──────────

Reflection How might you show yourself to be a beacon of hope in a chaotic work environment?

Action Write your belief in hope and how you apply it in your workplace. For example, "I believe that hope is something I share with people when they complain about how they are treated here by their bosses. I let them know they are important and that their work is well done." Or "I look for one good thing in each person I meet and share it." Then, each day for the next week, share your belief about hope with everyone you contact. One employee who used this exercise said she found that it "turned around my view of my workplace." She renewed her hope in others as well as in her own work, and she was recently recognized by her boss for her improved performance.

The Counselor of Hope

By spending time listening to others, sometimes I can help them discern where they are currently. This creates for them, I believe, a sense of hope and personal value.

JERRY NANNA, *WORKPLACE ANGEL*

When a colleague came to him for advice, Jerry Nanna was ready to help and offer hope as he had done with many others before. "I think he felt confident coming to me because I have enough gray hair," he says.

This time, his colleague, Tom, was asking for advice about the lack of internal job promotion. Jerry shared his unique perspective on how he helps others navigate the shifting sands of today's workplace. He encouraged Tom to move on, embracing the change as an opportunity to find a more suitable place to use his talents. Jerry had been down this path himself. For twenty years, he worked his way up in merchandizing and management to become president of Abercrombie and Fitch.

But he felt that he was not fully appreciated. So he reinvented himself and left retail, moving into management consulting and eventually into the financial services arena. Today, he is a senior vice president of a global insurance and financial services organization.

Jerry continued his conversation with Tom by asking him how he would entitle his biography if he were to write one today. When Tom did not respond, Jerry offered his: "Uncharted Waters." "My emphasis was on how we should be prepared for change," he reflects. "I have reinvented myself more than once in my life and wanted to let Tom know he wasn't alone in his challenge."

"Tom's story is still a work in progress," Jerry says; "to date, he is still undecided. He is like many people, yearning for appreciation. Money is not the most important motivator. It is a matter of his own personal integrity. He is trying to make some compromises and rationalize some of the realities that he is going to have to compromise on. Even if it is just a matter of hearing it from a friendly source, it is in his best interest to move on."

As Jerry sees it, his belief in the value of hope means that he gives back to others belief in their ability to be successful in the workplace. As a Christian in corporate America, he makes it part of his work to serve others in need during career transitions. He believes it is counterproductive for people like Tom to stay in a workplace that is clearly not using the depth of his talents. He adds: "We are returning to an era of self-sufficiency. I think *anybody* outside of ourselves has more objectivity, and therefore we need to constantly find colleagues and professionals we can trust to help us get the most out of our work lives. Tom's motivation for staying, I believe, is to win. He has that first- or second-generation mentality: the rugged individualist, to persevere at all costs."

Jerry feels it behooves people to understand that they should seek careers and vocations rather than jobs. He adds that because a vocation is a path, it therefore creates a journey. Viewed this way, changing and adapting regularly to new work environments is a lifelong process for us—a process we all should expect and ultimately embrace. He elaborates: "So you continue to run this race called your vocation or career. You also learn to make compromises. By spending time listening to others, sometimes I can help them discern where they are currently. This creates for them, I believe, a sense of hope and personal value."

Discernment involves gaining insight and perspective. It is a process that, Jerry has found, helps others gain a deep sense of satisfaction in their work lives. His process appears to resonate with others: "My sense of hope through grace was given through me and also through family connections. I have always tried to stay connected—to what is going on in my environment, in my community, and with my relationships. Staying grounded in your spiritual life gives you a backboard to bounce up against—a glass backboard because God can see you through it."

Jerry's counseling extends even further, beyond his organization to his church. For the past five years, he has participated in his church outreach ministry for people in transition in the workplace. Jerry and his fellow parishioners offer spiritual and emotional support to job seekers just entering or reentering the workplace as well as those retiring—and to their families, who are affected more than many realize. From anxious parents who are troubled by their college graduate's returning to live at home after an investment of many thousands of dollars in college fees, to a spouse trying to adjust to the new retiree now at home all day, Jerry finds himself constantly sharing the gift of discernment and hope. This is a gift that has brought him tremendous joy and satisfaction—a gift that shows how powerful hope can be.

——————— ANGEL REFLECTIONS AND ACTIONS ———————

Reflection What would the title of your workplace autobiography be? If it is not a hopeful title, how might you reword it to instill a sense of hope?

Action Write possible titles for your workplace autobiography if you were to write it today. In a few words, write what you would like it to say. Is there a difference between where you are now and where you would like to be? Help others work through the same exercise. What hope can you create for yourself and others to close the gap?

Hope and Success

Hope is the resource of the confident and the currency of the faithful.

NIDO QUBEIN, *WORKPLACE ANGEL*

To hope is to desire something, with some confidence of fulfillment. Hope is a grounding for expectation. A great example is people who emigrate to a new land with hope in their hearts, breathing success into that hope through their actions.

Nido Qubein came to this country in 1966 as a teenager, knowing no English and having no contacts. With fifty dollars in his pocket, he left his home in Lebanon, his culture, and his family to seek the American dream. Today, he is chief executive of an international consulting firm, a partner in several other successful ventures, and a board member of seventeen universities, companies, nonprofit organizations, and a bank.

An award-winning speaker and author, Nido addresses business and professional groups around the world. His high-energy performances inform, entertain, and inspire others to have hope. As one of the world's most recognized and respected business speakers, Nido is the youngest person ever inducted into the International Speakers Hall of Fame. He is the only recipient of his first alma mater's doctorate of law degree. In 1997, he received the Ellis Island Medal of Honor from the U.S. Congress, an award that honors immigrants and their descendants for their contributions to America.

Successful business ventures in real estate, banking, advertising, and consulting have given Nido the opportunity to be a model and mentor to many. He serves his local church, as well as community and charity groups, and continues to spend quality time with his family.

Having lost his own father when he was only six years old, he was raised by his mother and older siblings. With only a fourth-grade education, his mother planted the seeds of hope in his life. She shared with her children her "commonsense" philosophy that change comes from within. She encouraged her children to work hard, live life from the inside out, and make good choices regardless of their circumstances.

Here in the United States, Nido learned the English language by writing and defining ten new words each day on index cards and reviewing them all week long. While he worked hard and attended school, other major events helped mold his life and influence how he lived it. An anonymous physician picked up the portion of Nido's tuition bill that he was unable to pay. Nido vowed from that day forward that as soon as he made money, he was going to put others through college. At the young age of twenty-four, he started his scholarship fund, which is now underwritten by others who partner with Nido. Over the years, he has contributed all of the royalties from his books, audiotapes, videos, and other products to the Nido Qubein Associates Scholarship Fund, which has educated more than three hundred students to date. In 1997 alone twenty-nine students enrolled in various colleges and universities thanks to his contributions. He blesses others and offers hope by helping these young people earn their degrees. It is his way of giving back for all that God has given him.

Nido also felt the significant impact of his "mother in residence," an older woman on social security who lived in his dormitory. She chose to invest what little she had in him to help purchase the car he needed to continue his education while he was transferring to another school. "Out of adversity emerges abundance," he shares, adding that he learned about the joy of giving and the virtue of sacrifice from the physician and the housemother.

Hope is a journey of many steps. Nido shows people that even if each act is a small one, they accumulate and foster hope. Here are the "principles of hope" he offers to the thousands of people he works with annually:

1. Have a clear vision of your business. You need to grasp your position in the marketplace and know why customers do business with you.

2. Have a solid strategy for making necessary changes in your business and achieving your goals. You need a reliable "map" that indicates where you are and where you need to go. A balanced life is imperative. Divide your time equally between *earning*, *learning*, and *serving*.

3. Develop practical systems to achieve your goals. Solving problems, with outside help if necessary, can help you move ahead.

4. The best ideas, principles, or talents are useless unless they are executed consistently. Nido points to his own life and the consistent effort he put forth to learn seventy new words per week, which enabled him to become fluent in English.

His message stresses the value of *education*, which teaches people "why," as opposed to *training*, which teaches people "what." Training tends to be mechanical and quickly becomes obsolete with rapid change in the business environment. In contrast, education helps employees understand the reasons behind actions and policies, so they can respond effectively to new business needs.

To all of us in the workplace facing pressures from lack of time, money concerns, complexity of work, and accelerating change, Nido offers hope. He emphasizes that business leaders must motivate themselves and their employees to develop a mind-set that copes well with these pressures and welcomes the pace of change as a challenge rather than a threat. "Most of us would rather be comfortable than excellent," he remarks. "In today's business environment, comfortable people don't survive." By applying his four principles of success and emphasizing education rather than training for employees, you can put yourself ahead of the game.

If we are to live happy lives, we must be useful, honorable, responsible, and compassionate toward others. As Nido reminds us that we are warmed from fires we have not built and that we drink from wells we have not dug, we remember that there is great hope when we help build bridges that allow others to cross chasms in their own lives: "I'm living proof that the American dream is available to those who are willing to work hard and work smart, even if they start out as I did, knowing no one and having no money and no language skills. You just need to have the right principles and be willing to put them into action."

Nido continues to ask God why he has been chosen to receive so much in life. The answer is always the same: he is instructed to keep on giving to others. "What do you choose to focus on?" Nido asks us. "Is it to count? Is it to stand for something? Is it to make a difference? When we [shift our attention] from success to significance, our lives will be a blessing to others. Hope plays an important role in life's success. Without it, life would be reduced to aimless purpose. With it, all things are possible."

——————— ANGEL REFLECTIONS AND ACTIONS ———————

Reflection What is your history of hope?

Action Create a chronology of your life's experiences with hope. Draw a horizontal line across a blank sheet of paper. Place a 0 at the far left end and a 100+ at the far right end. Draw vertical lines that intersect the horizontal lines at varying ages up to the present. Mark the high points in your life where you held great hope for something. List the hoped-for things, rather than the actual things received. What does your chronology of hope reveal? Are you an eternal optimist? Do you turn your hopes into reality? Have you listed hopes for others, or just for yourself?

The Hope Maker

I have to keep believing that despite all the challenges there is hope. Everything is working toward a greater good. Instead of repelling adversity, I am learning to embrace it and look for the gifts within.

TOMASINA STEPHON, *WORKPLACE ANGEL*

Tomasina Stephon is called the "Hope Maker" by her alumni clients. As assistant director for alumni career services at the Northern Illinois University Hoffman Estates Education Center, she helps hundreds of college graduates find workplaces where they can thrive. "I'm very blessed that I get the opportunity to make a difference in peoples' lives every day," she says. The majority of people who contact her are unhappy with their jobs or careers, but when they work with her they are introduced to a world of hope.

"People share with me how lost they are," she relates. "They often say, 'I'm so alone and don't know where to turn to make a change. I'm dissatisfied with what I am currently doing. I don't know where to start.' It's not so much that these people want to find just another job. They want a job where they feel they fit—where they can use their education and skills supporting an organizational mission that helps make the world a better place. They say things like, 'Tomasina, I just can't get excited about selling widgets anymore.'"

Many of these people have experienced significant events that caused them to reevaluate what career choice works for them. Tomasina says, for example, that the birth of a child, the sickness or death of a parent, or reaching a notable birthday can trigger a reevaluation and quest for a higher quality of work-life balance.

In addition to all the career management tools and re-sources she shares, she offers hope as a powerful spiritual value that she herself embraces daily. When things get particularly difficult in the workplace, she asks God why she is being given certain challenges. Looking back, she realizes that those chal-lenges often act as bridges to new ways of understanding and empathizing with others: "When clients say, 'Tomasina, you understand me,' they're right: I do. I realize that because I have experienced so many ebbs in my life, what the famous speaker Jim Rohn calls the 'winters' of life, I can understand. These winters are down phases or valleys we all go through at one time or another."

Tomasina helps people reframe these events. Through hope, we move through this stage to a better place. She com-ments, "I think people really need to hear this. Sometimes, I need to say it more than once so it sets in—that there has never been a time when spring has not followed winter." One graduate used this advice to stay in her workplace, renewing her hope that even though she did not see her efforts reap re-wards immediately, her impact was being felt. Within a year, she was promoted and received many congratulations from her fellow workers, to whom she had offered hope through-out that time.

"I have to keep believing that despite all the challenges, there is hope," Tomasina comments. "Everything is working toward a greater good. Instead of repelling adversity, I am learning to embrace it and look for the gifts within." To her coworkers, she is always present, always sharing her hope. She unselfishly takes more time for others than she does for herself.

Besides being able to really listen and establish rapport, another gift that she has is a huge network of resources. "As a broker of connections, I'm often able to connect people with resources in the community they didn't even know existed. That gives people hope too."

"It's definitely a process and a journey—one that we are constantly revisiting." Tomasina recognizes the important role we can play in others' lives when we choose the path favored by this powerful workplace angel who clearly merits the title of "Hope Maker."

——————— ANGEL REFLECTIONS AND ACTIONS ———————

Reflection What have been the "winters" of your life?

Reflection How have these experiences deepened your ability to feel compassion and empathy?

Action Find someone who is going through a winter of life in your workplace. Remind him how spring always follows winter, and ask how you can assist him in coming to a spring of hope.

Building Hope

Lisa Badke is only twenty-five years old, but she sounds as wise as an old sage. She has deep feelings about the suffering of families with children living in deplorable conditions in the inner city. I first talked to her after I read a story about her in the local paper. She was so moved by the plight of a family living in an abandoned building during Christmas that she enlisted the help of many area merchants in donating much-needed items. After I finally tracked her down, I found out that this was not her first time helping families in need. Talking with her on the phone, I was impressed with the depth of her concern for others.

In a time when people go about their business, not recognizing others who may be in need, Lisa holds the belief of hope like a shining lantern in a dark, often scary world—hope that others will take her lead and do something on their own, not just talk about but actually get out of their comfort zone and make a commitment. As wonderful as it is to give during the holidays, all of these people still need assistance after December twenty-fifth has passed. Lisa is busy throughout the year doing for others; in addition to going to school to pursue a degree in social work, she is also a full-time nanny. One wonders where she finds the time to give of herself.

Her first experience of helping people was when as a junior in high school the national honor society held a canned-food drive. Teaming up with a partner, she set out to scrape up all the donations they could. She was most impressed and humbled by a family who, although they had little food of their own, insisted on making a donation when in fact they could easily have been recipients of the drive. To this day, she holds this family as a model of kindness and hope.

Lisa aspires to work for the Illinois department of children and family services after she receives her degree. Hoping to help kids who have fallen through the cracks, and doing this while they are young enough to effect real change in their lives, she says: "These kids can't be blamed for their parents' mistakes; they need a chance and an opportunity, and I'd like to be one of the solutions, not part of the problem. It's a shame to blame a child when they're so young. It's so easy to be a positive influence; it's amazing the good it could do. You do the best you can and remain hopeful that others will take your lead, and give of themselves a little."

––––––– ANGEL REFLECTIONS AND ACTIONS –––––––

Reflection Who has inspired you to have hope?

Reflection How can you emulate their example?

Action Read your local newspaper and list people in need of help, or organizations in need of volunteers. For each item on the list, write how you might personally help out. Choose the one list item and helping-out comment that most inspire you to action.

Hope and the Window with a View

When she first met workplace angel Bob Ganchiff, Thalia Poulos was new to Chicago. She had recently started a business in professional organization. Her concept was to become an efficiency expert for individuals; her client base consisted of two people: a commodities fund manager and an art gallery owner. She helped them organize and manage their desks, papers, files, and time. From her research on the new service economy, she thought that she had a service that would be in strong demand. However, she was unsure how to reach her target market.

Thalia met Bob through a mutual friend at a business function. She was immediately surprised when he asked her about her business; rather than responding as so many had before with comments like "Oh, that's nice" or "Why would anyone pay for that? They could do it for themselves," his reply was, "Hey, that's a brilliant idea, for today's world where there's never enough time!" In that first meeting, he sat there, intensely connected and supporting her by saying, "I know so many people who need that sort of service." He philosophized about time, our struggle with it, and how what we do with it forms the "essence" of our lives.

Thalia was mesmerized by Bob's way of thinking. She had recently been counseled on her startup by a nonprofit organization, where she was told that for the type of business she wanted to start she should go to every little shop in her local community and tell them she would type their letters. Bob was at the other end of the counseling spectrum: "Think big!"

Thalia was intrigued by Bob's enthusiasm for her then-innovative concept and wondered why it was so easy for him to be supportive. She learned that he had a gift for mentoring. He later shared a story about how as the head of recruitment for a major bank his large corner-office window had a view of the impressive Chicago skyline. Many applicants being ushered in for interviews reacted to the sight by saying, "Boy, what a view of the skyscrapers." That was not what Bob was waiting to hear. He was searching for applicants who would comment on the brilliant contrast between the lake and the sky, or the mixture of architectural styles—in other words, people who showed they think conceptually. He said the bank was searching for people who could see possibilities—people, he sensed, who had the ability to dream big. He was good at identifying these people; many did not come originally from the financial sector but were indeed able to fulfill their dreams in that kind of business.

Bob was Thalia's champion: "He really cared about me. He took a personal interest and followed up with helpful assistance." He gave her hope by encouraging her to stick to her business dreams. Today she remembers fondly conversations in which he showed her possibilities that others could not or would not see. He also supported her actively by calling his friends as potential clients and accompanying her on some visits. She found that Bob's network was made up of long-term personal and professional friendships; he knew other men like himself. From consciousness of the birds-of-a-feather theme, she became privy to the way men network—quite differently from what she had been used to in networking with women at structured, organized association meetings. She learned a new way to build business opportunities. Out of three appointments he took her to, two of them became long-term clients. With a number of new clients and a wonderful coach, she renewed her commitment to her dream.

When I mentioned Thalia's referring to him as a workplace angel generating hope, Bob was very surprised: "You never know what really sticks with people. For me, part of it is helping people who are more or less the 'underdogs.' I enjoy helping people reach their full potential. It is also great to just be there when others are in need."

Today Bob is a full-time career coach and business advisor, whose clients include many successful individuals and organizations. He develops hope in others just the way he helped Thalia: "You never know what is going to stick. We all need sounding boards and call-them-as-you-see-them coaching."

——————— ANGEL REFLECTIONS AND ACTIONS ———————

Reflection Prayer: Dear God, help me keep my values and hopes up throughout the day so that by the end of my workday I am at peace with myself.

Reflection What one thing gives you hope above all else?

Action What one thing can you do today to give hope to others? Once you know what gives you hope, you can give hope to others. For example, one young woman's hope was that her fellow workers would become more considerate to one another. Once a week for a month, she arrived at work before anyone else with a home-baked treat and set it in the lunch room with a note that said, "Renew hope in our workplace: do something unexpectedly good for others." She signed the note, "Your Anonymous Workplace Angel." She made sure she did not give away the fact that she was the originator of the good deed and watched throughout the next month as people started doing similar good deeds anonymously, along with smiling more, offering to assist others with administrative tasks, and even gathering more for lunch-time chats.

What Hope Can Create

Taylor once asked me, "How can people not see angels? They're everywhere."

TRICIA CRABTREE, MOTHER OF
WORKPLACE ANGEL TAYLOR MARIE (AGE SEVEN)

Here is a story that came to my Website. In it, a young child believes she has been called to bring hope into the lives of many others, both children and adults. The story is told by her mother, Tricia, who in addition to being a proud mother is also a great writer.

MY DAUGHTER, Taylor Marie Crabtree, started a business called TayBear Company. She earns income by making and selling hand-painted hair clips at local stores. When she started her business, I assumed that she wanted extra spending money, but then she told me the purpose of her business.

Taylor was going to use the income to buy teddy bears for children with cancer. She said the kids probably have a lot of sadness in their lives and she wanted them to have something special to hug and to hug them back. Taylor wanted them to know that even strangers care about them. She set her goal at buying and presenting five hundred teddy bears. I thought her too-high goal was that of a child who didn't really understand. *I* was the one who didn't understand.

The media picked up on Taylor's project, and our community has embraced her efforts. But help has come from far beyond our little community. Taylor has received cash donations from strangers who live thousands of miles away, just from word of mouth. It has been rather like a chain letter from the heart. In her scribbly second-grade handwriting, she wrote each person with her appreciation and an update on her project. She has also expanded her project to include over one hundred other children (including special-needs kids) as helpers. Taylor wanted other kids to feel that they too were capable of helping others in their own way. Along the way, she also raised her goal to presenting seven hundred teddy bears.

What is truly amazing is that she has sold over one thousand hair clips. She buys supplies over the Internet, and she has e-mail letters going between herself and the marketing directors of several large companies who offer advice. She keeps financial records of all donations, supplies, sales, and checking account activity (yes, she even has a business account) and has arranged for some corporate donations of money. The local supermarket even stuffs grocery bags with her flyers and has donation cans at their registers. I've listened in amazement as she's discussed the huggability of the teddy bears with vendors and later ordered seven hundred teddy bears after negotiating a lower price. She has been very clear that none of this is about her, but about helping the kids with cancer.

Taylor has been touched by so many people on her journey. While selling hair clips, one woman began questioning her about the project. She was very suspicious about just where the collected money was going. Taylor gladly talked on and on about all the little steps she had taken to that point, and about children and cancer. Looking on, I noticed that the woman's suspicions had turned to sadness. She became teary eyed and stopped Taylor in mid-sentence. She leaned down and hugged Taylor from a place deep in her heart. She told Taylor that her eight-year-old son had died just five months before from cancer and that he would have been very proud to have had one of her teddy bears.

Each day after selling, Taylor and her helpers talk about the people who had touched their hearts. Maybe it was the homeless man who had donated eleven cents and was surprised when he was told that was plenty of money to buy a hair clip. He and Taylor stood together choosing just the right hair clip for his lady friend. Or maybe it was the young woman who was flying back home the next day to say good-bye for the last time to her father, who was dying from cancer. Perhaps it was the man who drove all the way to his bank and back in order to buy a hair clip for his mom. He said that his dad had recently died from cancer. He wanted a child to have a teddy bear in his dad's memory. With each hair clip or donation have come so many memories and a realization that when working toward a goal from your heart, the journey too is part of the experience. Taylor once asked me, "How can people not see angels? They're everywhere."

Taylor likes to talk to people about her project. She gets suggestions, support, and ideas from just about everybody. Just when she is stuck with a problem, somebody gives her an idea to build upon. She says, "By talking to a lot of people I'm able to get more ideas than I could have on my own. I really learned a lot about running a business."

These are her suggestions for a successful project:

1. Believe in yourself.
2. Keep good records.
3. Try different things; it's OK to make changes.
4. Be very careful with your expenses.
5. Never, never give up.
6. Ask for help; don't try to do everything yourself.
7. Enjoy the little moments.

Taylor developed a rich hope for kids with cancer—the hope that they would be able to enjoy every day, no matter how many days they have left. For all the children, for all the parents, family members, and friends of those children, we thank Taylor for the hope she has brought to all those whose lives she has touched.

———— ANGEL REFLECTIONS AND ACTIONS ————

Reflection What is your formula for success?

Action Find someone with whom you can share Taylor's story. Think about starting a similar program on your own. The beauty of her story is how it keeps growing as it is shared. I passed the story on to a friend who had a little girl the same age as Taylor who was recently diagnosed with terminal cancer. I told Taylor, and she provided the little girl with a teddy bear. Taylor was touched by the little girl's story and asked to have a picture of her holding the bear so that she could "feel closer to the little girl," since she lives in a different state.

Angel Advice Corner

Bringing More Hope into Your Workplace

Here are some simple tips for bringing more hope into your workplace. Review them regularly for further direction in building the power of hope in your world of work.

- *Light the way of hope for another.* Hope lights the way for even the deepest doubter. Even if you cannot see someone shift from doubt to hope, you can still choose to offer others words of hope whenever possible.

- *Create your own acronym for hope.* A powerful acronym of my own is Helpful Optimism Promoting Equilibrium. A synonym for equilibrium is balance, a word that is very popular currently. Hope creates balance for those who own the belief because it outfits the owner with protective armor against life's hazards.

- *Give people hope by asking for their help.* It's amazing how people respond positively when you ask for their help. Asking says, "I value you and your assistance." I remember going around one of the offices where I was consulting and making specific positive comments. "Gee, Mary, you always have such a neat desk. How do you keep it so clean?" Of course, Mary would beam and proudly give me one or two tips as to how she kept her space so organized. Some people feel disingenuous giving compliments regularly. To me, it is part of creating a better place for all of us to work. What I have seen in twenty years is that people model others in their workplace. A workplace filled with people who genuinely acknowledge one another sets a foundation of growth and joy rather than isolation and fear. I have been in other places that are considered revolving doors: people go in and out every six or twelve months on average. I wonder why the management in those companies does not wake up and see the bottom line shrinking along with employees' attitudes. Empowering people is what this is all about. Empowering is letting their power out.

- *Laugh more often.* What things can you laugh at as a tool for moving past some challenge and into hope?

- *Create an "angel of hope charter."* On a sheet of paper oriented horizontally, make three columns. In the first, write the names of all the people who have inspired hope in you. In the second, alongside the person's name write one or two sentences describing how she or he gave you hope. In the third column, write one action you can take to emulate that person.

Hope: A Summary of Angel Actions

Give small doses of hope—through continual acts of caring—to others daily. Many donors of the Women's Opportunity Fund have shared with me that through giving they indeed renew their hope. Small things they take for granted, such as running water or a warm, cozy bed, become much-appreciated luxuries. In turn, they realize how important we all are in connecting to one another to offer hope through small, simple, yet effective acts of caring.

Write your belief in hope and how you apply it in your workplace. Then, every day for the next week, share your belief about hope with everyone you contact.

Write possible titles for your workplace autobiography if you were to write it today. In a few words, write what you would like it to say. Is there a difference between where you are now and where you would like to be? Help others work through the same exercise. What hope can you create for yourself and others to close the gap?

Create a chronology of your life's experiences with hope. Draw a horizontal line across a blank sheet of paper. Place a 0 at the far left end and a 100+ at the far right end. Draw vertical lines that intersect the horizontal lines at varying ages up to the present. Mark the high points in your life where you held great hope for something. List the hoped-for things, rather than the actual things received. What does your chronology of hope reveal? Are you an eternal optimist? Do you turn your hopes into reality? Have you listed hopes for others, or just for yourself?

Find someone who is going through a "winter" of life in your workplace. Remind him how spring always follows winter, and ask how you can assist him in coming to a spring of hope.

Read your local newspaper and list people in need of help, or organizations in need of volunteers. For each item on the list, write how you might personally help out. Choose the one list item and helping-out comment that most inspire you to action.

What one thing can you do today to give hope to others? Once you know what gives you hope, you can give hope to others. Remember the young woman who, hoping to make her fellow workers more considerate of one another, left home-baked treats in the lunch room with a note saying, "Renew hope in our workplace: do something unexpectedly good for others. Signed, Your Anonymous Workplace Angel."

Find someone with whom you can share Taylor's story. Think about starting a similar program on your own.

3
CHARITY

*Acting with Goodwill Toward Others—
at Home and Work*

> *Life's most persistent and urgent question is: What are you
> doing for others?*
>
> —MARTIN LUTHER KING, JR.

Charity is "an act or feeling of benevolence, goodwill, or affection." In 1941, Winston Churchill said that "the destiny of mankind is not decided by material computation. When great causes are on the move in the world, we learn we are spirits, not animals, and that something is going on in space and time, which whether we like it or not spells duty." Today our duty is to take a long look at our workplace and see where we can best serve.

Throughout the United States, thousands of individuals in countless workplaces are working to give back. Such well-known organizations as AT&T, Apple, State Farm, and Timberland have public service programs. For example, at Apple employees help children in hospital wards play computer games. Every AT&T employee is given one day's paid vacation each year for volunteerism. This adds up to thousands of hours of charity acts annually.

Charity, in the form of philanthropy and volunteerism, are part of our history. No sooner had the pilgrims arrived in the New World than groups of people started helping each other. People formed communities before they formed governments.

The spirit of giving has developed throughout the ages to the point that today businesses by the thousands are involved in structured giving programs like the United Way as well as volunteer programs that reach into local and national communities.

Yet charity also involves giving to others within our workplaces, through our time, dollars, and talents. As Ken Blanchard, best-selling author of *The One-Minute Manager,* states, "The best minute you spend is the one you invest in people." The word *invest* means more than just "to give"; it connotes giving with an expectation of yielding some benefit. Blanchard refers to the benefit being returned to the workplace. This harmonizes well with the meaning of the word *charity,* from the Latin *caritas* ("affection") and *carus* ("dear"). Later, *charity* took on the theological meaning of God's love for man and man's love of fellow man. Today it means, among other things, an act or feeling of goodwill. It does not limit itself, however, to just giving to the poor. Charity is put into action through the spirit of love. Love is the ultimate energizer.

Albert Einstein said that it is our obligation to put back into the world at least the equivalent of what we take out of it. Even so, many people feel they are *owed* something rather than that they owe. As a parent of two teenage boys, I am surprised by the number of times they tell me I must do something for them because I owe them that as a parent. Of course, I am confident that sooner or later they will outgrow this opinion!

In the words of Albert Schweitzer, "There is no higher religion than human service. To work for the common good is the greatest creed." He epitomized the essence of charity. Giving up a prestigious career as a doctor, he went to Africa to build hospitals for the poor. Tracked down by his friends, who felt he was throwing his life away, he was asked, "Why should such a gifted man as you give up so much to labor among African natives?" He replied, "Don't talk about sacrifice. What does it matter where one goes, provided one can do good work there?" He remained in Africa until his death in 1965 at the age of ninety. All the while, he maintained a dedication to serving.

Charity is service, giving the real gift of our time and talent as well as our treasure (the dollars we earn). Schweitzer's towering personal commitment to charity is a beacon for those of us courageous enough to follow.

Charity and the Mitzvah Team: Good Deeds

My employees feel like I care about them. This is where dignity and true charity come in. I also realize I am competing with companies that are charging less to their customers and simultaneously paying their employees less. But as I hold on to my employees, with almost zero turnover, it becomes clear that my customers will pay more for a higher-quality product and better service from happy employees.

CAROLE VOLMAN, *WORKPLACE ANGEL*

Carole Volman has her own charity team, whom she proudly calls the "Mitzvah Team." *Mitzvah* in Yiddish means "good works," and when it comes to someone understanding the power of good works in the workplace, that is Carole. Ten years ago, when she started her marketing development and telemarketing company, Strategies (in Rocky Hill, Connecticut), she brought her own special brand of workplace charity with her.

Her son Josef, an attorney in New York, referred his mother to me as a workplace angel. He mentioned that she had a special way of achieving success through dignity and caring. When I had the opportunity to talk with her, it was clear that those attributes have helped her create quite a successful business.

All her good deeds actually have some basis in her own "selfish" goals. As she puts it, "When you talk about good deeds, I think you also talk about selfishness. I'm selfish because I want good employees and know that by providing my employees with good pay, a pleasant and comfortable working environment, praise, and room for growth, they return my efforts tenfold." Bringing in bagels for her staff, making coffee, and even extending personal loans to employees are activities she includes in her job description. She explains: "My employees feel like I care about them. This is where dignity and true charity come in. I also realize I am competing with companies that are charging less to their customers and simultaneously paying their employees less. But as I hold on to my employees, with almost zero turnover, it becomes clear that my customers will pay more for a higher-quality product and better service from happy employees."

With a college-educated staff, Carole provides her customers with a successful team of bright and trained telemarketers. They do not work traditional eight-hour days, but rather six hours. This decrease goes a long way toward motivating employees; she has found results in higher productivity levels.

She also acts as a source of charity for the personal needs of employees: "Sometimes when you take your mind off your own troubles and elevate them to other areas where you can help others, you help yourself even more." For example, she hired someone who had some major legal problems, giving him an opportunity to start over again (though with some serious talking about what she expected of him). She adds, "Two years later, he is an outstanding employee. He was in a very high position elsewhere before he started here, but with us he had to start at the bottom. He made the best of the second chance I was able to give him."

When some young employees had problems paying back their college loans, Carole lent them the amount they were in arrears. She told them, "We are never going to discuss this again. When you have that money, it will be your responsibility to pay it back." To date, everyone has paid back their loans.

"You might think that I have a lot of money, but I am still in the struggling stages, investing back into my business," she emphasizes. "I have always held the personal sentiment that whatever you can do to help God on earth—even the small deeds you can do to relieve His burden—is what you should do. This also means doing whatever you can do to help others lead lives of dignity. You need to remember your real purpose. I don't believe my purpose is to become a millionaire. I want to live comfortably and leave something for my family, but you can't just plow over people."

As Carole puts it, she developed her belief in charity growing up in a warm and loving household; her mother's Yiddish sentiments live on with her in everyday matters. One of the words she uses often is *balabutish,* which means showing respect through your actions: "You have to get up every day and think about what that word means. It means to get up, take a shower, get dressed, and greet the day in a way that is respectful to God—and to yourself as well."

Her beliefs can also be seen in the high expectations she has of her employees: "You know how the dress code has been more casual these days? I don't allow that here. I believe you are performing a service that is dignified. The prospect sees you as you see yourself. If you are clothed in jeans and a T-shirt, you are not being respectful. You have to dress for success."

She drives home the importance of thinking before you act or talk, pointing out that "this requires effort and a concern for others and yourself. Sometimes people misconstrue your approach. They don't believe you have that much concern for others. Especially if you are nice to someone, they might construe that you are easy—that you don't have strict guidelines. But you don't have to abuse people to discipline them. I take a different approach to getting the job done. There are guidelines for caring. We have policies for everything, from the quality control of telemarketing calls to the cleanliness of the workspace. Each employee knows what he or she has to do to be successful, maintaining their dignity at all times."

For Carole, the process of charity involves building confidence and character, not production. She holds that charity is objective caretaking; it is about doing business while also recognizing the bigger picture of the power of charity in the workplace. "You can't save the world. But if you can touch people in a positive way, you can make a difference. I may be anxious about the growth and development of my business, but I am very much at peace with how I treat people. By doing things daily for others, you nurture your own soul in profound and powerful ways."

──────── ANGEL REFLECTIONS AND ACTIONS ────────

Reflection Who is part of your "mitzvah team"?

Action Think of some small monthly charitable gift you can give to honor your employees. At Strategies, Carole gives out movie tickets to the staff once a month. Of course, as Carole adds, "You have to take into consideration the affordability of your effort."

Finding Time to Connect

For me, opportunities to help others are everywhere.

MARY RODINO, *WORKPLACE ANGEL*

It is not unusual to find Mary Rodino sharing her business cards with almost anyone, anywhere, at anytime. From a backpack filled with kid snacks and other things for her two little girls, she pulled out a card to give to a young woman from Singapore standing in line with her at the Magic Kingdom in Disneyland. The visitor had recently graduated from school, and Mary thought she might be able to help her find a job.

Wherever she goes, she keeps her trusty business cards ready to pass out at all times to anyone she thinks she can help. What is surprising, though, is that this top woman executive, a regional head for a telecommunications company, takes the extra time to go out of her way to serve others. Another opportunity occurred when she was buying stockings at Nordstrom. As Mary tells the incident:

> I ASKED ONE of the employees, "Is there any order to this?" She said, "No, you have to just look through them. But let me help you." Within minutes, she had pulled out ten different colors that were my size. When she was finished, I thanked her and asked for her name. She said it was Helen. With that, she went back to work in the rear of the store.
>
> When my children and I were standing in the checkout line, I got to thinking about her and said, "I've got to talk to Helen!" I quickly grabbed my children and took off to find her. (You see, my children are used to me doing this type of thing.)
>
> I found her in the back. I said to her, "Helen, have you ever thought of working elsewhere? You did such a great job helping me. I might have a position for you." She replied, "I just don't think my English is good enough." I insisted, "I think you're English is just fine." I left her, remarking on a look of renewed hope in her dark, shining eyes.

I have known Mary for more than three years now, and every conversation we have is about praise for someone other than herself. She shows charity through her constant interest and involvement in improving the lives of anyone she possibly can. I believe she doesn't realize just how different her thought process is from others who are constantly self-focused.

People like Mary show us what true charity can mean in the workplace.

———————— ANGEL REFLECTIONS AND ACTIONS ————————

Reflection What weekly activities put you in a position to be charitable to others in your community?

Action For one week, take a look at the "everyday" people in your life: the dry cleaner, the restaurant server, the bagger at your grocery store. Offer a word of praise for each person with whom you connect. Do not be surprised if you find more blessings coming to you as a result!

Building the Charitable Profitable Business

D oris Christopher's company, The Pampered Chef, boasts a sales team of nearly forty thousand independent "kitchen consultants" selling gourmet kitchen items. You might think that with so many people working for her, she would be lounging at home or on a luxury cruise. Instead, she spends a great amount of time helping others. She began her business in the basement in 1980. Her high-quality products have led to recent sales exceeding $400 million dollars.

Doris became heavily involved in charity work through the inspiration of other companies. An example of her true goodness was to enlist the help of her field salesforce and customers in her charitable efforts. Six years ago, The Pampered Chef partnered with an existing program called Second Harvest, the largest food-based network in the United States with close to 185 network food banks. Second Harvest takes in surplus food from large companies and restaurants and sends it out to community shelters and food pantries across the country. By providing funds to Second Harvest either to buy additional food or support operating expenses, Doris and her organization are working to make sure that those in need do not go hungry.

Each year from September through December, The Pampered Chef hosts its "Round-Up from the Heart" program. At cooking demonstrations, called "Kitchen Shows," kitchen consultants ask their customers to round their individual orders of kitchen products up to the nearest dollar or more. The additional amount is then donated to the nearest Second Harvest network food pantry. In the program's first year, round-ups totaled $76,000. An average of $500,000 annually has been raised in the last three years alone. Last year, the company partnered with the Women's Opportunity Fund (which was spotlighted in Chapter One of this book), also providing donations from profits earned from product sales.

Doris's generosity is also tempered with wisdom and common sense. She explains that when she talks with her employees she focuses on letting them know they have done a good job and are appreciated. She recognizes that people need acknowledgment for their efforts, so she spends a great deal of time listening to and mentoring others. She believes that if you always deliver more than is expected by your customers, sales consultants, and staff, they will come to know that they matter. Her daughter Julie, who works in the business, has this to say: "I believe the most remarkable thing about my mother is that these philanthropic endeavors are something she would not imagine doing without. Her generosity is genuine and extends to a level well beyond 'token'—in fact, I believe it surpasses 'abundant'! Above all, my mother has taught me, by example, to recognize the needs of others."

The goodwill Doris extends to her employees and her community exemplifies the workplace angel of charity.

──────── ANGEL REFLECTIONS AND ACTIONS ────────

Reflection Where can you champion charity in your organization?

Action Team up with one or two other employees to champion a charitable organization like Second Harvest in your community.

Nancy Burgess, a photographer and community volunteer, did just that in her town of Long Grove, Illinois. Her efforts in growing a double crop of food, along with those of others in her town, have resulted in tons of extra food each year for those in need.

A Journey of Charity

The good things others do don't get publicized enough. It is so important to encourage people to carry their power—and that includes their charity—into their workplaces daily.

LAURIE DAVID, *WORKPLACE ANGEL OF CHARITY*

Laurie David grew up in a seemingly ideal situation. Her parents were able to build strong careers and a strong family life at the same time. She started out wanting to be a missionary and went to college ultimately planning on attending seminary. About halfway through college, however, she started working part-time at a local medical center in Jacksonville, Florida, in their human resource department. She recalls, "I decided to switch my major to business because I loved what I was doing in that part-time position. The hospital offered me a position after college, but I decided I wanted to work in a larger corporate environment. While working in a business setting, I realized that God needed missionaries in the workplace too."

Laurie says she was fortunate to find a great corporation to work at when she started at Sara Lee. Her first position there was as a compensation and benefits analyst. After two years, she moved to North Carolina and worked for the company in several different divisions, in HR positions. By her seventh year she was the director of employee relations, with responsibilities in Central America and the Caribbean. She later relocated to New York (and now Chicago) in executive-level positions, still with Sara Lee.

Laurie says, "I have been able to work with so many people and in many different environments. It has only reconfirmed to me that the business environment can be a mission field too. I have been absolutely sure that God wanted me to work in this environment, making a difference each day." She ended up spending three years in eight Central American countries. She says she will never forget her exposure to all the community-building initiatives supported by the company's local divisions. One special project involved providing sponsorship for a medical clinic in an underdeveloped community in the Dominican Republic: "We've built recreational facilities for schools, started up child care centers, and provided needed medical supplies and book programs, among other things. Our programs are very successful, and it's been so rewarding!"

Laurie emphasizes the great good she sees being done by corporations and their employees worldwide; "a lot of the people and employees who work with the company really care." She believes that the press does not always share the good things that are going on in underdeveloped countries thanks to corporations like the one she works for. As she sees it, the results come from building a foundation of honesty that employer and employees then share.

She adds, "You always have to please the shareholders, but there is room for great good for a great number. In working for a corporation like [Sara Lee], it is wonderful that part of your performance appraisal asks, 'What are you giving back to the community?' We help grow our employees, and giving something back is part of the exchange." She personally can say she has been involved in building the leadership of the organization. She is particularly motivated by being able to make a difference for people now as well as those who will be there long after she leaves. She has found that through giving back in a conducive corporate environment, we can all benefit greatly.

She currently works as the executive director of management planning and development, with key responsibilities including succession planning and development for the executive levels of Sara Lee's multiple companies. Her goal is to ensure selection, development, and retainment of leadership within the organization worldwide. This means she identifies and mentors employees who hold beliefs of charity and act on them consistently.

The bottom line for Laurie is that there is still a great deal of good out there. As she puts it, "The good things others do don't get publicized enough. It is so important to encourage people to carry their power—and that includes their charity—into their workplaces daily. We can really make it better most of the time. When I don't make it better for someone, or make it more difficult, I want to hit myself on the head and say, 'Darn, I missed an opportunity to make a difference!'"

———— ANGEL REFLECTIONS AND ACTIONS ————

Reflection How are you currently serving in your workplace?

Action Take on a leadership role. This is the advice of Lee G. Bolman and Terrence E. Deal in their persuasive book *Leading with Soul: An Uncommon Journey of Spirit*: "Organizations and institutions suffer and sputter when we ask too much of our leaders and not enough of ourselves. Effective leadership is a relationship rooted in community."

Action If anything were possible, what would you do to serve more in your workplace? Write three or four ideas, and place them in order of interest to you. Put them away for a day or two. When you revisit them, write possible steps you can take to initiate the first idea. Then take action on those steps. Go on to the other two or three ideas and do the same. One young man with good writing skills in a high-tech organization decided to offer a class on business writing for his fellow employees. The company has gone on to host regular skill-building classes put on by employees once a month.

Angels Often Do Not Realize They Are Helping Others

When you are able to touch another person's life . . . now, that means something!

CHRIS BUZANIS, *WORKPLACE ANGEL*

When Chris Buzanis was an executive at a world-class hotel corporation, she had a young female employee who was particularly difficult. For example, the relationship started off with her young protégée, Sue, leading Chris to believe she was older than her nineteen years. But Chris was patient and saw there was hope for Sue; she showed her how she could get ahead through being honest and caring. Throughout the time that Chris worked with Sue, she helped her advance in the organization. Eventually, Sue moved to another department and started working in sales, where she was very successful.

What makes a recent meeting of the two interesting is that Sue asked Chris, "Do you remember getting a number of cards from my parents when I worked with you?" Chris recalled the frequent cards, always thanking her for "being there" for Sue; she had never thought much about the cards before. "Well, what my parents didn't say was that they were thankful to you for even more than just helping me get ahead here."

"What do you mean?"

"Well, I never told you, but I had attempted suicide before I started working with you. But things changed so much after you took me under your wing. Each day, I would come in and you would have something positive and constructive to say about my performance. Every word of appreciation would act as a counterweight in my mind, pushing me farther and farther from the idea of suicide and closer and closer to the idea that I was not only worthy of living but could be successful as well! My parents could see that you played a large part in changing my life and were grateful for your kindness."

As Chris relayed this story to me and recalled how she had been shocked to hear it, I was touched by her reactions. She said: "I was having lunch with a top-level male executive from my workplace recently. He asked me, 'What would you say was your best experience here?' I responded with the story I just told you. This executive, however, didn't get it. His eyes just glazed over. Later I realized he had been wondering about something like my best job-based accomplishment here. I mean, when you look at what you've done throughout your working life—the deals you negotiated or the promotions you got—how does that really make a difference? But when you are able to touch another person's life . . . now, that means something!"

It is very clear that Chris has her priorities in life well ordered. What matters most is to have regular impact on the lives of others. Today, she continues to connect with others, looking for the next person to take under her large angel wings of charity.

——————— ANGEL REFLECTIONS AND ACTIONS ———————

Reflection Who can you take under your wing in the workplace?

Action Find someone you can take under your wing to support emotionally, as did Chris. Set up a weekly meeting with that person at which you receive progress reports and provide additional support. In each meeting, acknowledge any and all steps the person has taken.

An Angel Network

You have not lived a perfect day—even though you have earned your money—unless you have done something for someone who will never be able to repay you.

—RUTH SMELTZER

Charmaine Stradford saw the need for a program that would help African American employees advance at her company and decided to do something about it. Having worked at AT&T for nine years, she is now a branch operations manager. Like most managers, she works many long hours, but she still makes time to support the special alliance network she founded in Chicago, called "The Power of One."

The Power of One is a professional development network for African American employees of AT&T. It partners upper-level managers (typically African American but not necessarily) with those who would like to become managers. Charmaine is now the chairperson of the local chapter, and the cochairperson of the national chapter.

According to Charmaine, "The Power of One is truly a great opportunity for myself as well as other African American employees. I attempt to locate mentors who are geographically near their mentees, making it easier for them to get help when it is needed. The one difficulty I have had is finding African American mentors for all the mentees, but I have found upper-level managers very willing to volunteer as mentors."

There is also a path for current nonmanagement African American employees to become mentors. Charmaine has established requirements for these potential mentees, in a ten-course curriculum offered internally. Networking with AT&T's education and training department, Charmaine and her cochairperson decided what series of courses would assist in preparing nonmanagement employees for management positions. This coursework also required agreements with AT&T's internal unions. Everyone involved signed off, and the courses are now being offered within AT&T. The best part, though, is that they are free and held during the day. As Charmaine recognizes, "I think this is really great because people now have a path of development they didn't have before."

Charmaine took the extra time to do the right things that would move not only her own career forward but those of many others—a noteworthy act of charity. Ask yourself how you might create a similar opportunity in your organization. It does not have to be a minority network. It can be any sort of support network where there is a need. Even in some of the most backward organizations, I have found employees taking the lead on networks like the one Charmaine created. Learn from the success of others. Get started today.

——————— ANGEL REFLECTIONS AND ACTIONS ———————

Reflection If you could create a program to serve disadvantaged employees in your workplace, what would its objective be?

Action Find someone within your organization who can join you as a partner in championing a network like the one Charmaine helped build. Dean Foods, headquartered in Rosemont, Illinois, created a women's network to help their female employees advance. Menttium 100, a national mentoring organization based in Minneapolis, has helped thousands of middle-management women in hundreds of companies around the country break through the glass ceiling.

Support for Angel Work

Our true acquisitions lie only in our charities; we get only as we give.

—WILLIAM SIMMS

When Don Vlcek started working at Domino's Pizza, he was told that the president of the company, Tom Monaghan, said he shouldn't work weekends because "that's family time." He was impressed. Don was hired in 1978 as president of Domino's pizza distribution corporation, and he quickly realized he was working for a different kind of organization: "What a motivating thing that was for me! It was totally opposite of anything I had heard before." It was this kind of work-place atmosphere that furthered in Don the value of charity.

He accomplished some great acts of charity while he was employed at Domino's, acts that became the foundation for his successful book *The Domino Effect*. He tells of an incident that occurred in Denver. He was watching the weather channel and saw there was a blizzard heading toward Colorado. The weather bureau was predicting more than two feet of snow. He immediately thought of his truck drivers, who would have to drive through such conditions, as well as the thousands of residents who would be snowbound and in need of food.

Don had worked with his employees to be prepared for crisis situations like this. When the other local restaurants and grocery stores ran out of food after a few days, Domino's still had plenty. Don started getting compliments and national news attention, but he took it all in stride, saying that this was part of his job. As he puts it, "I didn't drive those trucks; I didn't risk my life on icy highways; I got compliments, but they were going to the wrong source. I passed them on to my employees, who deserved them."

He worked diligently during his years at Domino's to instill in others the belief in charity. He recalls seeing some of his regional managers developing egos, taking power away from others. When he saw his lower-level employees losing motivation, he decided to do something. At their next awards banquet, rather than give awards to white-collar management, he gave additional awards to blue-collar workers.

In the 1980s, Domino's was the fastest-growing large company in the United States. But a definite decline set in with the Pizza Wars. Don found himself having to lay off people who had worked for him for as long as ten years. He did not like that and decided to leave. Monaghan had fired his executive team twice—all except Don Vlcek. But the company was in financial trouble. As Don puts it:

I EMOTIONALLY FELT it was time to go, but Tom had given me such an opportunity and support I felt I couldn't leave him. Then my daughter decided to go live with her mom, my ex-wife, in California. I couldn't sleep. I was throwing up. I missed my daughter terribly. She told me she could come back on weekends and we would have just as much quality time because I was busy during the week at Domino's. I found myself having more and more difficulty going into work. At 10:30 one morning I said, 'God, please send me a message telling me what to do,' because I didn't know whether to stay or leave.

Two and a half hours later, while visiting with my best friend at his home, we suddenly realized his little three-year-old girl was not around. We found her face down in the family hot tub. She had accidentally wandered out on her own and slipped in. All this happened in just minutes. We called for paramedics immediately, but we were too late. She fell into a coma. The next day we pulled the plug on her. The message I had asked for was now crystal clear.

Don felt a calling to change his working life—to create more time with those special people in his life, especially his daughter. He also wanted to share his knowledge of the importance of charity in the workplace with as many other organizations as he could. Today, he is a sought-after speaker and consultant, working out of Plymouth, Michigan, helping organizations build healthier, more charitable workplaces. He takes his work seriously, but he also remembers that charity must begin in the home.

———— ANGEL REFLECTIONS AND ACTIONS ————

Reflection What can you do today to balance your life so that you have time to do what is really important to you?

Action Heal the hearts of others. Look for opportunities to be of service to others who are suffering. Consider everyone your extended family. Give people the benefit of the doubt. Even if they look as though they need no one, it is at that very moment that they probably need you most. When you look at those who are great leaders, you see that they are always giving their time and charity to the suffering, especially those called "the walking wounded," the millions of us who are hurting but still walking through our daily routines.

Ask Yourself Who Is Being Left Out

Charity brings to life again those who are spiritually dead.

—THOMAS AQUINAS

Workplace angels *include* people in their worlds. They share their hopes, dreams, and fears with others. They also share their time. Have you ever experienced loneliness in the workplace? How about rejection?

I remember a female colleague of mine (we'll call her Marsha) calling me in tears a few years ago. She was crying because the members of the class she was attending, other new trainers like herself, had basically ostracized her at the session lunch break. This was the second day of training, and she had assumed she would lunch with the same people as on the first day. She told me that she had stopped to get some money at a cash station and was with another of the class attendees, named Susan. Both Marsha and Susan had asked the group to save them seats at the restaurant where they would all be eating. But when they arrived they found the group had saved a seat only for Susan. Not one person in the group tried to find another chair. Instead, one of the group said, "Why don't you just sit at that table next to us?"

Marsha looked at the adjacent table. It seemed miles away from where the group was sitting. She looked back at the group, blurted out "Forget it," marched back to the hotel where the class was being held, and called me. I listened, hurting so much inside for her, knowing myself what rejection feels like. She was too hurt to follow my recommendation simply to finish the class she had been enjoying up to that point. I said she should at least leave the teacher a note and tell her honestly what had happened. She did so and then went home and slept for the whole afternoon.

When she had time to reflect on the experience, we both agreed that we were not the first to have experienced a lack of caring. We vowed as trainers ourselves to watch out for people in the classroom, to make sure that no one felt left out. I thought about all the times I might have unknowingly left someone out of an activity. I now keep this in my mind whenever I am with people, making sure that others are included in conversations.

Who might you connect with today to help him feel more included in your workplace? Do you have an orientation for newcomers? If you do not, why not volunteer to create one? You would be surprised at the number of companies that do not have orientation days. How can your employees help your customers feel welcome in your place of business if they have not been properly welcomed themselves?

It always surprises me, in working with hundreds of different organizations and thousands of people over the last fifteen years, to discover that these simple things can profoundly change our work environment. They are influential way beyond the hundred-thousand-dollar strategic plans that often get shoved away in drawers, and the expensive training sessions, and the occasional motivational celebrations. It is really the day-to-day, little, positive changes that add up to eventually shift first the hearts and then the minds of those at work. Charity is not just about giving when it is quite evident that someone is in need. It is a matter of constantly *being on the lookout* for people who might need support.

―――――― ANGEL REFLECTIONS AND ACTIONS ――――――

Reflection Who is left out of your daily activities with colleagues?

Action Find someone in your work area who is currently being left out. Spend some extra time with her. You might find she has valuable things to share.

―――――――――――――――――――――――――――――――

Charity, a Winning Strategy

We are starving for something more, something beyond success as we move toward the next millennium. We no longer want to simply make a living; we want to make a difference—to make contributions that extend well beyond ourselves.

BRIAN BIRO, *WORKPLACE ANGEL*

As Brian Biro, an expert on workplace satisfaction, has discovered, for some people developing a satisfying workplace environment is a real chore. According to him, many people blame others for their unhappiness. Thus, rather than create positive change, they generate a never-ending cycle of complaints.

Brian is the founder of CLASS (Coaching, Leadership, and Synergy Services). Brian has many insights into the new needs that are rising like an epidemic in the workplace: "We are starving for something more, something beyond success as we move toward the next millennium. We no longer want to simply make a living; we want to make a difference—to make contributions that extend well beyond ourselves." His emphasis on belief in charity—acts of goodwill and caring for one another—is clearly seen in a story he enjoys telling:

I WAS RECRUITED by Lynden Air Freight at an extremely difficult time for the company, when the majority of its business was oil-related. The company had built a strong position in a specialized niche, providing air freight service from the forty-eight states to Alaska. Just before I joined the company, the OPEC cartel in the Middle East made decisions that sent the price of oil plummeting. Overnight, the price had fallen more than twenty dollars, to less than ten dollars a barrel. Oil-related construction immediately slowed nearly to a standstill. So did the bulk of our air freight business.

I was brought on board to assist with strategic planning and productivity enhancement—just before every employee in the company took a cut in pay. In the two months prior to my being hired, several individuals had lost their jobs, because of the sharp downturn in business.

As I listened to the people in the organization, it became apparent that their central focus had shifted to the outside, away from factors they could directly influence. Virtually every business conversation centered on the depressed marketplace, decreasing cargo space to Alaska, and the bottom-line question of whether there would be any jobs tomorrow.

The president of the company was a person of energy and vision. He was willing to take some risks to ignite positive change. At a time when most leaders would disdain so-called extra expenses for personal development training, new marketing campaigns, enhanced systems for measurement and communication, and incentive compensation opportunities for all employees, he was ready to take action. He allowed my team to implement an ongoing communication program focused on shifting the mind-set of our entire organization away from what was happening to us from the outside to what we could make happen on the inside.

The results were astonishing. Every aspect of the organization improved dramatically and rapidly. Over the next three years, the company nearly quadrupled its sales while diversifying its customer base by opening several new market niches. Even more important, internal recognition and acknowledgment became a constant in the organization as teammates expressed their genuine appreciation for one another.

For the first time in its history, Lynden received national recognition as a leader in customer service and convenience. Through a simple shift in focus, every member of the organization felt more consistently successful. People viewed themselves as valuable contributors to a quality team.

As Brian emphasizes, supporting others is how he reaches true success. He recognizes the all-important force of a team that is structured of individuals supporting one another.

——————— ANGEL REFLECTIONS AND ACTIONS ———————

Reflection What would you do to bring charity into the workplace during a crisis?

Action Find someone in your workplace you can team with to build charity through communication. Whether it's an informal team meeting or just one-on-one sharing of thoughts, ideas, and actions on charity, every day you can share your belief in giving. For example, whenever I help another and am thanked, I always add, "You're very welcome. I only ask that you do something similar for someone else, as I did for you." By adding this one phrase, you build a true spirit of passing on charity throughout your workplace.

Angel Advice Corner

Bringing More Charity into Your Workplace

Here are some simple tips for bringing more charity into your workplace. Review them regularly for further direction in building the power of charity in your world of work.

- *Give to others.* If you give to others, you receive more confidence in yourself.

- *Be willing to include others in your world.* For example, Jeri Sedlar tells of her friend Andrea, who gives out angel pins to those she recognizes in her workplace.

- *Keep giving.* There are all kinds of simple, charitable things that we can do for others every day. Think of what kinds of things make you happy (a funny card, a phone call, a sincere compliment), and then share them with someone else.

- *Be a charitable soul.* We should all think of ourselves as charitable souls—great resources to others.

- *Remember the "angel rule."* The angel rule is "*Give* unto others as you would have them *give* unto you."

- *Give real gifts.* What is a real gift? Your time and talents, as much as your treasures.

- *Throw a fundraising party.* I have a good friend, Mollie Cole, who hosts an annual holiday party called "It's a Wonderful Life." The sign in her front yard reads, "You are now entering Bedford Falls." Mollie asks everyone to bring a food donation for a needy group. If you follow this suggestion, consider adding to that a five dollar donation for a children's charity. Use the story line of the famous movie, as Mollie does, to play out the theme of charity to others. You will have fun and make a difference at the same time.

- *Set aside special days for community events.* Schedule a special day in your workplace for employees to volunteer in their respective communities. For example, AT&T gives all of its employees one paid workday annually for volunteering. I have spoken with many employees at companies with initiatives such as this and have consistently found it to be a great morale booster, as well as wonderful p.r. for the organization.

- *Be creative.* How about doing what one manager at a Chicago-area Humana Hospital did: bring in lottery tickets for all his employees? The best part of the charitable act was that one of the employees won. It is also good to note that she shared her winnings!

- *Practice continuous caring.* In addition to random acts of kindness, consider continuous actions of caring and connection.

- *Get involved.* Applied Materials teamed up with the nonprofit Do Something to lead corporate America's involvement with youth-focused organizations and programs. Applied Materials has committed $1.25 million over the next several years toward making the nonprofit's Kindness and Justice Challenge a popular, annual program within American schools. Do Something is a national organization seeking to inspire and support young people of all backgrounds to take problem-solving action in their communities. It is Do Something's vision that young people across the country routinely take thoughtful and directed action to build measurably better communities.

- *Volunteer.* Volunteerism makes good business sense, whether your company employs five or five thousand. It gives your company the opportunity to help others, build teamwork among its employees, and enhance its reputation in the community.

- *Create a mission to make a difference.* Bob Gabrielsen is director of retail banking for Premier National Bank, an upstate New York business with $1.6 billion in assets. Bob's mission within his organization is to make a difference in the lives of the 325 people who report to him. The bank "walks" its mission statement; as he adds, "My belief is that every department in every business should first look at themselves as a nonprofit. By doing this, you create an explosion of ideas, of creativity. We do this all the time. We come up with things we can do, like creating consortiums to help small businesses and building strategic alliances." He shares the story of a man who came into the bank one day. The banker who served him talked about the company's mission, emphasizing his desire to make a meaningful difference in the man's life. The executive never asked the man how much money he had; he just continued sharing his passion about all the things the bank was creating to serve its customers. After two hours, the man said, "I can't believe you never tried to sell me anything. I have four hundred thousand dollars I am just coming into, and I'm going to be your customer for life." Bob concludes, "A lot of banks boast about having a sales culture. We boast about the next evolution, having an advisory culture. The difference is the focus on the customer. We're here to help people."

How many moments do you remember in your life that really matter to you today? If you are like most people, your answer is "Only a handful." If you embrace this thought, you quickly realize that the small details consuming your attention daily are just a backdrop for those revealing moments when you connect with others—as they make a difference in your life and you make a difference in theirs.

Here is my manifesto:

I live in faith, hope, charity, courage, truth, trust, and love every day. I forgive freely and graciously. I appreciate constantly and completely. I savor the glory of each hour, the holiness of each day. I respect the wisdom of others. I recognize the continuous opportunities to serve. I embrace joy as my ever-present companion. I cherish my existence and am eternally grateful for the love of others for me and for our world. I am at one with God.

Now write your own manifesto:

Charity: A Summary of Angel Actions

Think of some small monthly charitable gift you can give to honor your employees (within what is affordable). Recall that at Strategies, Carole Volman gives out movie tickets to the staff once a month.

For one week, take a look at the "everyday" people in your life: the dry cleaner, the restaurant server, the bagger at your grocery store. Offer a word of praise for each person with whom you connect. Do not be surprised if you find more blessings coming to you as a result!

Team up with one or two other employees to champion a charitable organization like Second Harvest in your community. Recall the efforts of Nancy Burgess in her hometown of Long Grove, Illinois, through which many tons of food were grown for those in need.

Take on a leadership role. This is the advice of Bolman and Deal in *Leading with Soul*: "Organizations and institutions suffer and sputter when we ask too much of our leaders and not enough of ourselves. Effective leadership is a relationship rooted in community."

If anything were possible, what would you do to serve more in your workplace? Write three or four ideas, and place them in order of interest to you. Put them away for a day or two. When you revisit them, write possible steps you can take to initiate the first idea. Then take action on those steps. Go on to the other two or three ideas and do the same. Recall the example of the young man with good writing skills whose offer of a class on business writing for his fellow employees led to his high-tech company's scheduling regular monthly skill-building classes.

Find someone you can take under your wing to support emotionally, as did Chris Buzanis. Set up a weekly meeting with that person at which you receive progress reports and provide additional support. In each meeting, acknowledge any and all steps the person has taken.

Find someone within your organization who can join you as a partner in championing a network like the one Charmaine Stradford helped build at AT&T. Dean Foods, headquartered in Rosemont, Illinois, created a women's network to help their female employees advance. Menttium 100, a national mentoring organization based in Minneapolis, has helped thousands of middle-management women in hundreds of companies around the country break through the glass ceiling.

Heal the hearts of others. Look for opportunities to be of service to others who are suffering. Consider everyone your extended family. Give people the benefit of the doubt. Even if they look as though they need no one, it is at that very moment that they probably need you most. Great leaders are always giving their time and charity to the suffering, especially "the walking wounded," hurting but still walking through their daily routines.

Find someone in your work area who is currently being left out. Spend some extra time with her. You might find she has valuable things to share.

Find someone in your workplace you can team with to build charity through communication. Whether it's an informal team meeting or just one-on-one sharing of thoughts, ideas, and actions on charity, every day you can share your belief in giving. For example, whenever I help another and am thanked, I always add, "You're very welcome. I only ask that you do something similar for someone else, as I did for you." By adding this one phrase, you build a true spirit of passing on charity throughout your workplace.

∞

4
COURAGE

Choosing to Face Obstacles Bravely and Helping Others Face Their Own Obstacles

I have found that the greatest help in meeting any problem with decency and self-respect and whatever courage is demanded is to know where you yourself stand. That is, to have in words what you believe and are acting from.

—WILLIAM FAULKNER

Courage is a matter of choice. As obvious as that concept might be intellectually, it is difficult to grasp emotionally. Faced with an ogre of a boss, the threat of losing one's job, a lawsuit, missing an important deadline, or countless other real and imagined workplace terrors, we do not feel as though we have the choice to be courageous. In addition, the current work environment makes many of us feel like victims. Because of the pace of change, we feel helpless and put upon. If downsizing does not get us, transfer to some outpost on the other side of the globe will. It is hard enough to find courage within ourselves. How then can we transcend our fears and help others in turn find their own courage?

If we take a moment to reflect on the reality of the workplace today, we realize that we are more empowered than ever before. In many organizations, empowerment is not just a word but a growing part of the culture. More people than ever are included in decision-making processes and allowed to use their ingenuity and leadership on cross-functional teams. Even more significant, however, is self-empowerment; I have observed it in people who work in every conceivable industry and at every level. As our society becomes more open and as individuals raise their consciousness through the spirituality movement, therapy, Internet communities, and in other ways, individuals feel a surge of personal power. They are much more willing to take risks, fight city hall, or take on scary issues than they were in the past.

I know this from my interviewing. As you will see from the stories that I share with you, there are many angels out there with the courage of their convictions. These people have chosen to be courageous. They could just as easily have chosen to be victims. To paraphrase René Descartes's famous saying: I choose, therefore I am. Each of us has the choice to be courageous in our workplace, and it does not matter if that workplace is as totalitarian and unspiritual as a former communist regime or a command-and-control corporation of the old style.

When I was twelve, I chose to be courageous. Growing up in a very dysfunctional home, I took the role of martyr until I reached the cusp of adolescence and declared to my mother, "You aren't going to hit me anymore." I realize that some victims of physical abuse find that words do not stop the beatings, but for me, they worked. From that time on, my mother no longer slapped me as she had done daily since I was little.

Looking back on the thirty years since that incident, I still wish I had stood up for myself sooner. I am as guilty as anyone of forgetting that it is a choice we can make at any time. Customer service representatives often forget they have a choice. They put up with an unreasonable amount of abuse and are terrified of confronting awful customers. But it can be done. As one customer service person at the safety equipment company First Alert once said, "When someone calls me who is obnoxiously rude and abusive, I say, 'I'm sorry, sir, but you cannot talk to me that way. Please talk to me nicely or this conversation will end soon.'"

Of course, there are situations where your only choice—and the most courageous one—is to leave. I have helped some people make just that choice. Some are takers and continue to take from you and give nothing back in return for as long as you let them. It is up to you to walk away from the relationship and not blame yourself. Saying "I quit" takes courage when you do it on principle, when you stand up for what you believe. Before concluding that leaving is your only choice, however, read through this chapter and see if you discover other options.

Workplace angels who tap into their courage do so at a price. Some even go through "the dark night of the soul." But they emerge stronger and more certain of themselves. Their acts not only inspire others but send a clear message that these are people not to be trifled with. They earn tremendous respect, which carries them forward in their jobs and their careers. They achieve a spiritual freedom that helps them rise above the fear that sometimes entraps us.

The Other Side of Courage

Sometimes we are needlessly afraid of being fired. Other times, we are *realistically* afraid of getting the ax. Both fears exert equal force on our actions and attitudes. Both cause many people who work to be cautious, meek, anxiety-ridden, secretly cynical, and silent. When fears rule your workplace and your life, existence is meaningless and unfulfilling.

Here are some of the most common fears:

- Ridicule
- Job loss
- New job responsibilities

- Poor performance review
- Conflict and confrontation
- Loss of income (pay cuts, withheld bonuses, etc.)
- Boss or bully
- Dealing with problematic subordinates
- Changes in company culture

As you have seen, the people profiled in this book manage first to be courageous in the face of these fears and then to pass on their courage to others with whom they work. Angels who espouse courage in the workplace are usually selfless role models for others. All of us have this capacity for courage. People who act bravely and heroically, however, are able to draw on inner resources that triumph over external villains. They draw strength from their beliefs; they trust their instincts; they define and adhere to their values. The stories that follow show varying aspects of forceful belief.

Anyone can be courageous in a work setting. Courage is a skill set that can be learned and deeply embedded in our response systems. Much more like endurance than beauty, courage is something anyone can develop and sustain. Most people, however, simply stop short of fully growing and realizing their courage.

As children, we saw a variety of courage tests and response patterns demonstrated by those around us. We learned and assimilated certain facets of those patterns to develop our own personal pattern. The good news is, if you learned deep messages about resilience, fortitude, optimism, and courage, you probably have a ready trigger for accessing those subconscious patterns when the need arises. If you were taught other, less rewarding patterns, your brain is blindly hardwired with the same amazing precision, but in a different direction. Yet even if your pattern makes you shy away from courageous acts, you can rewire your brain. The workplace angels I've interviewed all "feel" the courage within themselves. Whether or not this is a conscious process, they are able to reach down and find the confidence and conviction necessary to act upon their most noble thoughts. The stories, reflections, and actions seen in this chapter can bring more courage into your life and the lives of others. Many times, what seems impossible becomes doable if we simply know that others have gone before us. The workplace angels of courage help you along the way.

The Courage to Choose Community Interest over Self-Interest

Courage is not about doing something without fear, but about taking any strength you have—even if it is just a grain of courage—and channeling to strike out into the unknown when you know that what you're doing is morally and ethically right.

MARIA ARZA, *WORKPLACE ANGEL*

Maria Arza was hired by a respected national public relations firm to help save the Hispanic account of one of the company's oldest corporate clients. She was able to do so because of her ten years' experience in, and (by being Hispanic) her intimate knowledge of, that market. She was then assigned to be the supervisor of that same account for the client, a multinational fast-food corporation.

The client's goal was to increase its presence in the Hispanic market. As Maria learned more about how the client operated and the issues that the Hispanic community had with the client, it became clear that there was a major point of contention between the client and the community. Maria explained: "My client always used appropriate ethnic p.r. firms for the various markets but did not do the same for the Hispanic community.

The Hispanic community was absolutely adamant that this showed the client's lack of respect and commitment to the growth of the Hispanic market." Even though Maria was Latina herself and the community had no quarrel with her work, there was a problem in that her employer was a general market firm. The fast-food corporation did not seem to understand how deeply the issue affected its ability to achieve the goal of increased presence and market share.

As a result, Maria felt that she must make a series of recommendations, the first being that the Hispanic portion of the account be reassigned to a Hispanic p.r. firm—even if it meant writing herself out of a job. Following her convictions, Maria wrote an eleven-part memo to corporate management that included her strong recommendation to move the business to a Latino public relations firm.

Sacrificing her job for a principle required great courage. But Maria saw a real opportunity for her community, and she was convinced that it was more important to give something back to it than to keep a job. She knew she would find another job, but she was not sure if she would ever have so great an opportunity to give something back to people she cared about.

Maria explains: "I have only one face—this one. It is so important that my reputation stay intact. As my parents said, 'You are only as good as what is inside you.' When we landed here, all we had was what was in our heads.'" Another motto Maria follows comes from her mother's words: "You are not better than anybody else; but also, no one is any better than you." This motivated Maria to take responsibility for making the most of her life.

How was Maria able to make her heroic sacrifice? What gave her the courage to put her community before her own job? "My courage came from knowing this was the right thing to do. Also, this was the path the client needed to take to go to the next level: hiring an Hispanic public relations firm."

Maria knew that although such a firm did not currently exist, it could be born out of corporate need. Her organization was certainly large enough to fund it and foster growth within that industry niche. Choosing to provide better job opportunities for her community was, for her, the right thing to do.

Many of us think we have no courage. Part of the problem is that we see it in the same way we perceive beauty, as something disconcertingly elusive, sparingly bestowed by nature, and fleeting. For these reasons, we admire and even envy courage in others, but we are unsure we can manifest it when needed; instead, we recall how we failed to demonstrate it at some critical moment in the past. We admire courage because it translates posturing, speeches, and brave thoughts about one's foes or fears into action. Despite this admiration, we often shy away from situations that call for courage, afraid our words might exceed our deeds and we will not have what it takes to act.

This is a shame. A workplace act of courage energizes and enriches us. Even if the "worst" happens—if our brave deed results in termination—we can live to fight another day. For many people, it is a revelation that they can stand up to a cruel boss, or refuse a plum assignment that means uprooting their family. Suddenly, they realize that they do not have to be victims or passive members of their workplace. This is when people experience their power; it is when they stop viewing themselves as pawns and instead believe they are individuals who have an impact not only on their own lives but on those of others at work. Maria learned this lesson and modeled it in her decision to do the right thing.

——————— ANGEL REFLECTIONS AND ACTIONS ———————

Reflection Who in your workplace has shown the kind of courage Maria showed?

Reflection What steps could you take today to develop courage in your workplace?

Action Do one small, brave thing. You do not have to confront the CEO, become a government whistle-blower, or quit your financially remunerative job and join the Peace Corps. We can commit small acts of courage before we dare large ones. Each day in every workplace, there are opportunities for small, brave things. Maybe it is to get up a petition protesting a company policy that allows people to smoke in common areas. Or telling a subordinate politely and with care about an irritating habit. Or moving between two people who are sniping at each other in a meeting, to draw their fire so their argument does not rage out of control. It may be helpful to make a list of small things you might do (perhaps derived from "cowardly" moments in the past; the list would be the opposites) and keep it handy.

Courage on the Fast Track

Courage and perseverance have a magical talisman, before which difficulties disappear and obstacles vanish into air.

—John Quincy Adams

A certain corporate executive, "Dan," is a fast-track executive at a major corporation. With an MBA from a top business school and a resume that includes time served at a leading consulting firm, he was quickly moving up the company's ranks. Yet he was not particularly happy with his job. Not that he was unhappy, exactly; he received challenging assignments, got along pretty well with the people he worked with, and felt his compensation was more than adequate. Still, he felt the work had become routine. It was difficult to put his dissatisfaction into words. All he knew was that when he first joined the company he was caught up in the process of learning new things and proving himself. Now, he was at a point where he missed the freshness of new assignments and environments.

When he shared these feelings with friends, they told him he was nuts. He was just going through some early midlife crisis; he had a great job, and his disquieting feelings would soon pass. Dan took their advice and kept working hard, but the feelings stayed with him. One day, he entered an executive staff meeting; the topic under discussion was a possible downsizing. It seemed to him that the downsizing—or "rightsizing," as everyone was referring to it—was a fait accompli. From other meetings where decisions were clearly heading in a certain direction, he was acculturated not to rock the boat. Building consensus was almost a reflex; it was just the way things got done in organizations.

Yet this time it was too much for him. Dan came from a blue-collar background; his father had worked on a General Motors assembly line and been laid off twice. Dan still remembered how tough those times were on the family, both financially and emotionally. Perhaps this was why he now spoke up against the downsizing. It was not easy. His voice shook a little, and he stumbled over his words. Soon, though, his fervent belief in what he was saying took over. Dan made an eloquent case for alternatives to downsizing: voluntary retirement, temporary cutback in spending on new technologies, moratorium on pay increases, reduction in work hours. While admitting that revenues were soft and that the analysts were breathing down their necks, he admonished everyone in the room for looking at the presumably easiest solution to the problem, without weighing the cost in human hardship and suffering.

After the meeting, his mentor (an executive vice president) took him aside and chewed him out. He told Dan that if he felt strongly about the issue, he should have made his feelings known privately, in one-on-ones with key members of the executive committee. What he had done, his mentor continued, was disrupt the meeting and leave a sour taste in everyone's mouth.

Dan did not like the chewing out, or the implication that his action might have a negative impact on his future with the company. At the same time, however, he felt better about himself than he had in years. He was energized and excited. He immediately began working on a paper outlining strategic alternatives to downsizing, staying late every day for two weeks to get it done, and submitted it at the next committee meeting. Two weeks later, the committee decided to curtail any downsizing initiatives. Dan found himself receiving a hefty number of handshakes and hugs.

During the next four years, there were a number of other opportunities for him to act on what he believed, rather than to give in to his anxieties or what was politically expedient. Some of these opportunities were relatively minor; one involved his decision to cover for a subordinate who needed to take time off (time she did not have, according to company policy) because of a family matter. Still, he found himself with newfound joy in coming to work. He never knew when he would be given a chance to do something courageous, but he loved it whenever the chance arose. His entire outlook on what he did for a living changed.

As Dan puts it, "I may not be helping my career with the company by standing up for what I believe in, but I'm helping myself and other people I work with in ways I never could have conceived of before."

─────── ANGEL REFLECTIONS AND ACTIONS ───────

Reflection What would you do if your organization announced a strategy for cutting expenses similar to the one Dan encountered?

Reflection What one thing can you speak up about today that would help bring about a better workplace for all?

Action Create a one-page plan (no need to write much; simple bulleted points will do) for how you would like to respond courageously to a crisis. For example: "I will respond to a crisis calmly, looking for opportunities to turn the negative into a positive. I will help others work through similar crises." Having a plan in preparation (like a disaster recovery plan for organizations) helps you respond rather than react to the crises we all experience at one time or another in our lives. Being prepared even helps us thrive, not just survive, these downturns.

Going Up After Being Down

What people will value the most is your courage to face reality in all its messiness. Yet you must continuously have the intention to actively search for the good in everything. Had I not been challenged in such an extraordinary way, I would never have had the opportunity to live my life's purpose.

ANITA BRICK, *WORKPLACE ANGEL OF COURAGE*

Anita Brick's life is a legacy to her belief in courage. Here, in her own words, is the story of how she turned a tragic experience into the bedrock of a vocation.

WHY ME? Why was *I* crushed by that elevator? Why had this disaster come just when life was getting good again, twenty-two months after Tony, the love of my life, required emergency brain surgery to prevent an abscess from killing him? I've struggled with these questions for the last seven and a half years. What I've concluded is, "Why *not* me?" If I can triumph over these back-to-back traumas; fight through fear, sadness, and anger; build a positive new life after losing my home, career, and independence; and provide others with hope through my story, then why not me?

People say that the bigger the obstacle, the bigger the benefit. It's true, if you make the effort to find it.

This all started on February 16, 1990, when I left my apartment in downtown Chicago on a cold, blustery, winter evening to meet some friends. Several of us got into the elevator—unaware that it was broken.

Arriving in the lobby, three people got off ahead of me. Then, as I exited, the lobby doors slammed in my face. The doors attached to the elevator car stayed open, leaving me half in and half out of the car. All at once, we plunged down one and a half floors—my body skidding against the shaft wall, burning my left side and leaving huge purple bruises from my arm on down.

The elevator suddenly stopped, with the top of the car pinning me against the concrete shaft wall. My skull would have been crushed if not for the quick response of another passenger who immediately pressed the emergency stop button and used his cell phone to call 911.

At first, I naïvely thought I could just climb out, but my left leg was pinned and the pain was horrible. The massive elevator had stripped the flesh from my leg nearly down to the bone and was pressing my ribs into my lungs. I could barely breathe, yet I realized I was trapped and screamed, "Get me out of here, I'm going to die."

Somehow I had the presence of mind to think: it's time to rely on my faith. And so I did.

The rescue squad of more than a dozen firefighters arrived in only minutes. I remained hopeful, until someone yelled, "I've never seen anything like this before. What should we do?" I was stunned. I used a Buddhist mantra meditation I practice to keep myself calm and focused. I prayed that the paramedics would do the best job of their lives to get me out of there.

The team leader reached down and felt nothing but the muscle tissue that had traveled from my thigh up to my waist. He feared that moving the elevator to free me would kill me, sending my legs and internal organs to the bottom of the shaft. Fortunately, I didn't know that at the time. I remained hopeful and conscious and continued praying.

The Chicago Fire Department and the rescue squad did a terrific job. They got me out in about thirty minutes. I am deeply grateful for their quick reaction and the "Jaws of Life." Without them, I likely would have died. In the ER, I could tell from people's comments that I was in *big* trouble. But I kept focused on prayer, love, and the things I wanted to contribute in this life. I was not ready to die.

Just out of intensive care, the paramedics surprised me with a visit. They wanted to see how I was doing and learn how I had remained calm. I told them I chanted the mantra "nam myoho renge kyo," the "law of cause and effect," which gave me a positive focus when all else was chaos. "You know, it probably saved your life," one of them said. "You didn't panic, flail around, or lose consciousness. You helped us help you."

Their work paid off, yet my pelvis looked like it had been hacked up by an axe. Ten-inch surgical pins imbedded deep into my pelvis stuck out through my stomach. In later surgery, doctors implanted a rod and screws, which remain there today. Originally, doctors told my parents I'd probably lose my leg and not walk again.

Yet my surgeon, Dr. Armen Kelikian, saved both my life and my leg. He did a superb job. When my parents came to visit from New Jersey, my mother kissed his hands and brought him homemade strudel. Astonishingly, we discovered that Dr. Kelikian's late father helped care for my father in London, during War World II.

Some things I had previously taken for granted were now literally out of reach. Others became complicated, frustrating, and painful. Laughing was agonizing. So I let everyone know that when I wiggled my left index finger I was chuckling inside. Even a gentle hug from my father made me scream as he forgot and accidentally pressed on the screws in my pelvis.

But there were good days, too. While still a patient, I convinced the Rehabilitation Institute of Chicago to allow us to produce three episodes of "No Matter What." This cable television show, which my boyfriend Tony and I had started producing two years before, profiled individuals who triumph over obstacles. Despite my despair during these times, I felt empowered again.

By actively involving myself in others' lives—people who seized their courage—I was inspired to help others do the same.

I interviewed people who gave *me* courage. One was a five-year-old girl who had just lived through her twenty-seventh surgery—the one that would eventually enable her to walk. Another was a man who had been struck with twenty thousand volts of electricity that burned off his arms and legs. He would regularly "make his day" by encouraging others in the hospital. Our efforts won the 1990 statewide award for noncommercial public affairs programming. It was a great honor.

As I look back, I've gained a deeper sense of mission. Last August, I founded a new business, the Encouragement Institute. We help others achieve their goals and dreams. Often people dial our number to listen to that day's encouragement message; I originally wrote them to cheer myself up.

This year Anita shared her experience with one thousand participants at a women's conference. In addition, in 1997 she accepted the position of director of career and corporate alliances at the University of Chicago Graduate School of Business to bring her knowledge base, communication skills, and humanism into the lives of executives.

Today, Anita is in the process of developing a complete kit for those going through challenges to their courage. One of her most sought-after products is a tailor-made journal designed to address your unique challenge. Her three-part technique for tapping into your courage is potent; here she shares what she calls the Courage Quotient:

1. Consistently challenge yourself. You can have adverse circumstances and gain value from them if you have the courage to find the value for yourself and others.
2. Give yourself and others peace of mind. Search for solutions, to internally polish your character first, and then refuse to blame others.
3. Reward yourself and claim the victory. The only way to overcome challenges and get people to value you is to have the

courage to really dig and find the things you value about yourself.

Anita adds that when you value yourself you see your environment start to reflect that valuing: "What people will value the most is your courage to face reality in all its messiness. Yet you must continuously have the intention to actively search for the good in everything. Had I not been challenged in such an extraordinary way, I would never have had the opportunity to live my life's purpose."

We learn from Anita that courage comes through having faith, creating value in everything you do, and sharing your love and compassion with others. Even one kind word can give another person the will to live. It was true for her. She teaches us that courage is not a solo operation. Courage has to emanate from you, but it needs to be fostered and encouraged by others with whom you come into contact. Think of the word *courage*. It comes from the French word *cour* and the Latin *cor,* which mean heart. To encourage someone is to give them courage to help themselves and others. Anita has certainly made a vocation out of her courage.

─────── ANGEL REFLECTIONS AND ACTIONS ───────

Reflection What bravery have you seen shown by others in your workplace?

Reflection Who can you acknowledge today for showing bravery that could lead to sharing wisdom from the experience?

Action Make two columns on a sheet of paper. In one column, create an inventory of the ten most difficult times you have had in your life. Beside each item, write one positive outcome that resulted from the challenge. After you complete the exercise, look for patterns. Do you see themes that continue to play throughout your life? What statement of your courage do your challenges reveal?

Action Create a "joint-courage bank account." Everyone's call to courage is unique. Something that challenges you may not phase another person, and another person's challenge may seem simple for you to overcome. This is why Anita created the Encouragement Institute: to motivate herself at a time when she needed it and to help do the same for others. Building a joint-courage bank account gives other people courage when they need it, and vice versa; furthermore, in giving courage to others you build a reserve within yourself. On a sheet of paper, write the names of three people who need encouragement. Beside each name, write one encouraging thing you can do for that person in the next week (make a phone call, send a card, send e-mail, etc.).

Action From Anita also comes the idea to buy an extra copy of a book that encourages you and give it to someone who needs encouragement. Write an appropriate note inside the front.

Courage Is Not a Solo Operation

The best soapbox is a corporate soapbox. If you can do something that produces good results in the corporate world, more people will try it.

DEBORAH DAGIT, *WORKPLACE ANGEL OF COURAGE*

Deborah Dagit has a great talent for building trust. How does she do it? As director of diversity of Silicon Graphics in Mountain View, California, her title alone carries great clout. Yet she uses the one tool she knows has the greatest impact: her own body. Standing four feet two inches, Deborah, in the politically correct term, is "short-statured" and uses her size to disarm even the most resistant group. Her height does not get in the way, however, of facing issues boldly and directly; rather, it becomes the catalyst for addressing differences. For Deborah, outer appearance is one of the tools she is able to use to heal her workplace.

A good example of how she creates an environment of trust happened recently. Deborah launched a diversity initiative focusing on the significant percentage of employees in her organization from India. Optimizing the contributions of these employees in the workplace had not been easy. Managers and employees were having difficulty communicating effectively with each other. In addition, other employees were unaware of Indian customs. Along with a great deal of tension between Indian and non-Indian employees, there was an increasing turnover rate among the former group, who felt that the company was not sensitive to their needs.

Deborah started to heal the divisions by bringing in an expert on India to talk to employees about Indian customs and history. Then Deborah asked a panel of five Indian employees to talk about their experiences of U.S. culture. People had the courage to share what was most challenging in their new work environment and what they found different from India. Their candor opened up conversation with the audience. From this initial dialogue, people began to learn to value their differences. It opened up people's eyes as to why there were communication breakdowns.

Her program has significantly reduced the attrition rate at the company and set up continuing processes for keeping dialogue open. She has since used the same process for their new employees from the Asian-Pacific area and Russia. What she is doing takes guts. By encouraging dialogue between groups that view each other with suspicion, she risks conflict and confrontation. She also risks being called Pollyanna, someone too naïve and idealistic to realize that good intentions do not accomplish much. Deborah's courage is rooted in her belief in people and their ability to share aspects of themselves in a safe environment.

"Being short of stature has afforded me a unique vantage point," she says. "While I'm looking up, the person looking down achieves a unique circumstance to think about." Although there are approximately eight million short-statured people in the world of every ethnicity and cultural heritage, Deborah has found significant challenges inherent in day-to-day living in a world where many people judge others by their size. She points out: "Reactions range from those who seem delighted to see me, as if they have just discovered a leprechaun, to people who are afraid, believing me to be a gnome-like being who has jinxed their path. Finally, there are those who experience an insatiable curiosity about the most mundane aspects of my life, like where I buy my clothes, what size shoe I wear, or if I drive a car. Whether I'm in the grocery store or giving the keynote address at a business conference, I must be prepared to address these reactions."

Today, Deborah carries a great deal of power in her position at Silicon Graphics. She uses that power to show others that we all matter, we're all different, and those differences can serve all of us in creating a better world if we only celebrate the richness of our many perspectives. As she sees it, "The best soapbox is a corporate soapbox. If you can do something that produces good results in the corporate world, more people will try it." Deborah has found a great forum for her ideas in the world of business and brought along the courage to deliver the messages.

─────────── ANGEL REFLECTIONS AND ACTIONS ───────────

Reflection Where are your role models of courage (like Deborah Dagit)?

Reflection What can you learn from their experiences?

Action Assemble a group to start building a more connected workforce by sharing information on different cultures. One organization I worked for had an international potluck luncheon, where employees tasted different ethnic cuisines while watching *National Geographic* specials on various cultures.

Overcoming Handicaps

Courage is what it takes to stand up and speak; courage is also what it takes to sit down and listen.

—Winston Churchill

A good example is when I was told I would never be able to see again. At that point I thought, 'What the heck am I going to do? But then, at some point, forty-five minutes later, I felt a sense of joy. There are times like that when I realize things could be much worse. I definitely think it is a gift from God, but I don't know how it's done. What's amazing to me is the ability to change a point of view without changing my circumstances.

Dean Hudson, *WORKPLACE ANGEL*

Dean Hudson and Gayle Robison are similar to many people in the workplace. They get up daily, travel to work during rush hour, and spend their days dealing with problems that arise throughout the computer industry. Dean works as an access technology specialist, while Gayle trains people to use computers. The two have worked together for several years and have great respect for one another. So what is different about these two?

First, let me offer a clue. Sensory Access is an organization in Palo Alto, California, that provides employment opportunities for the visually impaired. Dean was born with what is termed "low-partial vision," which means that he was functionally blind until, at age twenty-one, he lost all his vision. Gayle's sight effectively ended when she was a college student. Today Dean travels the world, taking vacations by himself; Gayle is a mother and wife, actively involved in her community as well as her workplace.

Dean has been interested in computers since he was thirteen, when his father bought one for the family. Even though he was discouraged from using it, Dean soon arranged for the computer to take up permanent residence in his room. His love for computers eventually led him to obtain a degree in programming. He worked for IBM for three years developing speech technology; he left the organization in a downsizing. He was then at a crossroads, when he received a job offer from the Sensory Access Foundation. He had gone through many challenges, discovering that it is very difficult to work blindly in a world of sight. But he found a home at the new organization, which is dedicated to helping the blind become successfully employed.

Gayle helps teach Sensory Access applicants how to use braille, speech, or screen-enlargement programs at various client sites. This allows access to computer applications such as e-mail, report writing, spreadsheets, and database operations. Her blindness came from retinitis pigmentosa, a very slow-acting disease; she had full sight until her sophomore year in high school. Having been a champion badminton player in high school, she tells the painful story of how as a junior she was playing in a competition but within just a few weeks could no longer see the birdie. She hid her disease for many years until it was too difficult to go on doing so. Over the last twenty or so years, she has adapted. She was introduced to computers by her son when he was a sophomore in high school, but she never thought the tool would lead her to a new way of living and working. Today, at age forty-nine, Gayle has only one to two degrees of vision left, but she is able to see she has many opportunities still available.

Neither Gayle nor Dean makes a six-figure salary. They work at the Sensory Access Foundation because they feel they make a difference there. Dean says of Gayle: "One of the things I like most about Gayle is her wonderful sense of humility. She never asserts herself over others. She is also very forgiving. Those are qualities that won't get you promoted per se, but it makes the work environment better for other people to grow. I believe you never grow by people telling what they did wrong. What is more productive is having someone show you the right way. And then there is all the bubbly cheer that comes with it."

For Gayle, Dean is a wonderful asset in the workplace: "One of the things I love about Dean is his joy. He walks around our office singing. We're lucky, because he has a good voice! But seriously, you don't find that many happy people. I also see the courage he has to keep going in life. He goes and does things I would never do, like traveling to London and Amsterdam by himself last year. He constantly reaches out to others and shares his experiences, frustrations, and suggestions with them."

Dean adds, "I think I got my hope and courage from daily living. For some reason, from what I've been told I have a gift for letting go of terrible experiences. I can remember a couple times when I thought if I didn't wake up the next day, it would be okay with me. A good example is when I was told I would never be able to see again. At that point I thought, 'What the heck am I going to do? But then, at some point, forty-five minutes later, I felt a sense of joy. There are times like that when I realize things could be much worse. I definitely think it is a gift from God, but I don't know how it's done. What's amazing to me is the ability to change a point of view without changing my circumstances."

Whereas Gayle and Dean have become accustomed to working with sight challenges, many of us who have our vision cannot imagine where we would get such courage. The new world of work is creating places for wonderful people like these two, people who have so much to share and show all of us about how courage leads us to value everyone's contributions.

————— ANGEL REFLECTIONS AND ACTIONS —————

Reflection What could you learn every day if you saw with more than just your eyes?

Action Take one day and focus on your senses other than sight. Pretend that you cannot see, and connect to your other senses to tell you the truth of what is before you. Build the courage to share with people what you admire in them that might not be evident just from looking at them. From this vantage point, share from your heart what you see that really matters to the individuals with whom you connect.

The Courage to Grow

Courage, it would seem, is nothing less than the power to overcome danger, misfortune, fear, injustice, while continuing to affirm inwardly that life with all its sorrows is good; that everything is meaningful even if in a sense beyond our understanding; and that there is always tomorrow.

—DOROTHY THOMPSON

We're not just making a pretty little garden here; we're saving lives.

CATHERINE SNEED, *WORKPLACE ANGEL*

Catherine Sneed, a counselor at the San Francisco County Jail, was sure that her home garden had helped her survive a life-threatening illness. She thought the power of the soil might also work on her clients at the jail, mostly drug dealers and users.

Catherine convinced the county sheriff to let her create an organic garden on land adjoining the jail. She got prisoners out of their cells to restore an old greenhouse and to grub brambles from the site. At first the Horticulture Project had no tools, so the prisoners yanked blackberries with their bare hands. She begged tools and seeds from local merchants, but she was still short of money, gardening experience, and models for what she wanted to do. The jailers thought she was flaky, especially when she pushed the jail's kitchen staff to serve soothing peppermint tea from the new garden.

But jailer hostility receded as they saw prisoners become enthusiastic gardeners, bringing their zest back to the jailhouse at the end of the day. Some also brought spare seedlings, which they shared with guards, who became home gardeners themselves. Soon there was a waiting list of prisoners eager to join the program.

In short order, the Horticulture Project was harvesting tons of produce every year for the jail, for Project Open Hand (founded by a "Giraffe," Ruth Brinker; more on this in a moment), and for the soup kitchens of St. Martin de Porres. But the production of food is only a side effect of the Horticulture Project. Catherine says, "We're not just making a pretty little garden here; we're saving lives."

She teaches life lessons from the garden. The prisoners with drug problems see how well the plants grow without chemicals. Many of them have lived on junk food; now they see plants flourish with proper nutrients. They discover the tastes of fresh vegetables, because she cooks them lunch from the garden. Caring for small farm animals gives them experience in nurturing; planning the garden shows the benefits of long-term thinking; and physical labor pays off in visible, edible results. But the most powerful lesson is that mistakes in life, like those in the garden, can be corrected.

Catherine knew that, upon release, her "students" ended up right back in the places where they first got into trouble. A bridge program was needed, so she and some former inmates cleared a trash-filled lot near the Bayview housing projects and built the Carroll Street Community Garden. This is the home base of the Garden Project, a combination of counseling, work experience, and job training. Graduates of the jailhouse garden live in two drug-free homes at Carroll Street while they work and train in the garden, go through treatment programs, and attend school. They move on to employment on a third initiative of Catherine's, the Green Teams, which contract with businesses and the city to do tree planting, gardening, and community cleanups.

Catherine points with pride to the rearrest record for her gardeners, which is a quarter that of other former inmates, and to the huge waiting list for her not-flaky-at-all programs. Knowing the power of the gardens to transform both individual and community, she's pushing hard to accommodate the long waiting list of prisoners, and to build community gardens in lots all over the city. "I believe in miracles," she says, "but I can't wait for them to just happen."

Her story is just one of more than eight hundred showcased by the Giraffe Project, a wonderful program that since 1982 has been showcasing everyday heroes of courage. The people whose stories are spread by the project might not have displayed their courage in the workplace. Still, I want to mention them because they give lie to the belief that good deeds go unrecognized. More and more, groups like Giraffe are springing up to catalyze and honor displays of courage.

The Giraffe Project is so named because it encourages people to stick their necks out for the common good. The organization believes that the world needs people with vision and courage—people brave enough to put their ideas and ideals to work solving such problems as violence, hunger, and pollution. The project has been finding such people since 1982 and telling the stories of the "giraffes" to the nation. The project's members know that good ideas and good hearts do not solve problems if people are idle, and that the best way to move into courageous, caring action is to show them someone else who goes first. When people hear and see the project's stories of people taking on tough challenges in their communities and beyond, they are inspired to take on the challenges they face.

The project places Giraffe stories in media. They have been on all the major television networks and on the Voice of America. Radio scripts on Giraffes have been narrated by volunteers who include Candice Bergen and Sam Waterston. Giraffes have been featured in hundreds of local and national publications. People inspired by Giraffe stories have generated projects large and small, from cleaning up wetlands to housing the homeless. The project's files are full of messages from Giraffes themselves, confirming that its work has brought them vital encouragement, credibility, contacts, and resources.

The Giraffe program curriculum helps build courage, caring, and responsibility in kids from six to eighteen years old and then guides the kids in designing and implementing their own service projects. The school program is now in forty-seven states. The project has formed Giraffe program alliances with Cities in Schools, the YMCA, YWCA, Boys and Girls Clubs, and the U.S. Navy. Program partnerships allow private companies and service groups to sponsor the Giraffe program in their local schools and youth clubs. Television programming, speeches, and workshops are some of the other Giraffe activities. I have had the personal pleasure of working with the team at Giraffe headquarters in Langley, Washington. They are dedicated to showing the world the power of belief in courage, and their results speak for themselves.

——————— ANGEL REFLECTIONS AND ACTIONS ———————

Reflection Can you stick your neck out for someone today?

Reflection Who in your workplace has stuck his or her neck out for someone in need?

Action Involve your organization in a Giraffe Project school program today. By making a difference in a child's life, you alter how you look at your working life. Call (360) 221-7989.

Angel Advice Corner

Bringing More Courage into Your Workplace

Here are some simple tips for bringing more courage into your workplace. Review them regularly for further direction in building the power of courage in your world of work.

- *Do not give your power away.* Say what you need and want in life. Draw an invisible line between yourself and others if they attempt to take away your courage—your power. Realize you are safe behind the line and you have a choice: you can choose to take care of yourself first. After you say what you want, you can help the other person get what he wants.

- *Be open to others' ways of seeing the world.* When you hear something that does not sit well with you, ask yourself if you are uncomfortable because the idea is different from yours or because it is morally or ethically wrong. The latter situation is an opportunity for a courageous act.

- *Draw strength from alliances.* Nowhere is it written that you have to be brave by yourself. Think about alliances (unions) with those of like mind, in or out of your workplace. Use the strength of your common values and ideas to gain support, both verbal and in action, for the risks you take.

- *Think of courage as persistence.* I have great courage knowing that no matter what goes wrong in my life, I will never give up.

- *Look at the value in every valley you encounter.* In her book *Faith in the Valley,* Iyanla Vanzant writes about the "valley of value." It is a wonderful book for people who are seeking the courage to get through troubled times.

- *Inject humanity into a situation where people are acting like automatons.* Too often, those around us forget their human side and behave like cold, calculating professionals. It is risky to remind people that underneath the patina of professionalism lurks a generous and caring heart, but this is a risk that can make everyone feel better about themselves. Try what one employee at a major marketing firm did during a tense negotiation session in which people were being extremely harsh, ungenerous, and inflexible. She suddenly plopped a picture of her niece on the table and said, "Have you ever seen a more beautiful child?" At first the room was dead silent. The eight people in attendance, all men, just gawked at the non sequitur action. After a minute, however, one of them fished out his wallet, pulled out his daughter's picture, and put it on the table too, saying, "Well, take a look at my pride and joy!" Soon most of the men had taken out family pictures. The atmosphere changed dramatically, the very human emotions carrying over into the business negotiation.

- *Identify a situation at work where you acted like a coward.* Perhaps you failed to defend another employee who you felt was being criticized unfairly. Maybe you avoided an issue because you knew it to be a political hot potato. Perhaps you sat idly by while fellow supervisors made denigrating (racist, sexist, ageist) comments about people you work with. Why did you act in this fashion? What fear made you act this way? If you had to do it over again and could act bravely, what would you do or say?

- *Ask your coworkers what fears they have that prevent them from doing what they feel is right.* Perhaps they are afraid to confront a customer or to quit their job. It may be that they are afraid to go to workshops and conferences by themselves to drum up business. Lend them moral support. Explore their fears with them and brainstorm how they might overcome them. I worked with someone who was terrified of going to cocktail parties and other business functions; she was just terribly shy. I volunteered to accompany her to a few of these functions and give her support if she needed it. After the second or third time, she discovered that she could network and form relationships with the best of them. I felt great that I had helped her out, and she felt terrific about discovering a strength she did not know she possessed.

- *Acknowledge your current state, even if you are ashamed or embarrassed by your fears and cowardice.* When you recognize, you awaken. You become aware. You make different choices—better choices; you break away from limitations. You have more options, and the more options you have, the easier it is to make decisions. You become more flexible and open to opportunities. You *cocreate* them with others if only you allow your courage to emerge from your fears.

- *Realize that all change requires behavior modification.* Because we fear being criticized, most of the decisions we make are lukewarm. But if you move to a point of courage, you do not fear the outcome. You have faith that the outcomes reveal your earnestness.

- *Read* The Adversity Quotient *by Paul Stoltz.* He shows us how courage is, as Mark Twain stated, "resistance to fear, mastery of fear—not absence of fear." You will not be void of fear when you choose courage; rather, you find yourself moving with it, respecting it, not resisting it, understanding that fear is part of the process of owning courage and the opportunities that come with it.

- *A prayer for courage in the workplace*: Dear God, grant me the courage to take the initiative in making a difference in my work today. Help me champion those in need. Help me stand up for what I believe is right. Amen.

Courage: A Summary of Angel Actions

Do one small, brave thing. You do not have to confront the CEO, become a government whistle-blower, or quit your financially remunerative job and join the Peace Corps. We can commit small acts of courage before we dare large ones. Each day in every workplace, there are opportunities for small, brave things: create a petition protesting a company smoking policy; tell a subordinate politely about an irritating habit; separate two people sniping in a meeting. List small things that are the opposite of "cowardly" moments in your past, and keep the list handy.

Create a one-page plan (just bulleted points) for how you would like to respond courageously to a crisis. For example: "I will respond to a crisis calmly, looking for opportunities to turn the negative into a positive. I will help others work through similar crises." Preparing your own "disaster recovery plan" helps you respond rather than react; thrive, not just survive.

Make two columns on a sheet of paper. Inventory the ten most difficult times you have had in your life, and beside each item write one positive outcome from the challenge. Then look for patterns. Do you see themes that continue to play throughout your life? What statement of your courage do your challenges reveal?

Create a "joint-courage bank account." What challenges you may not phase another person, and another person's challenge may be something you can easily overcome. Recall Anita Brick's Encouragement Institute, created as a joint-courage bank account. List the names of three people who need encouragement, and beside each name write one encouraging thing you can do for that person in the next week (make a phone call, send a card, send e-mail, etc.).

From Anita also comes the idea to buy an extra copy of a book that encourages you and give it to someone who needs encouragement. Write an appropriate note inside the front.

Assemble a group to start building a more connected workforce by sharing information on different cultures. One organization I worked for had an international potluck luncheon, where employees tasted different ethnic cuisines while watching *National Geographic* specials on various cultures.

Take one day and focus on your senses other than sight. Pretend that you cannot see, and connect to your other senses. Build the courage to share with people what you admire in them that might not be evident just from looking at them. From this vantage point, share from your heart what you see that really matters to the individuals with whom you connect.

Involve your organization in a Giraffe Project school program today. By making a difference in a child's life, you alter how you look at your working life. Call (360) 221-7989.

TRUTH

Speaking Honestly,
Directly, and from the Heart

The search for truth is in one way hard and in another way easy, for it is evident that no one can master it fully or miss it wholly. But each adds a little to our knowledge of nature, and from all the facts assembled there arises a certain grandeur.

—ARISTOTLE

Workplace angels tell the truth constantly, caringly, and eloquently. "The truth shall set you free" is an apt phrase, since these angels are freed from the need to be devious and deceptive; they do not need to waste huge amounts of energy concocting excuses and explanations that conceal rather than reveal the truth. Their commitment to honesty adds weight to their words; no one doubts them when they say something; no one thinks they are operating with hidden agendas.

People want to hear the truth. They are tired of CEOs who mislead them about the company's future and bosses who try to manipulate them with white lies and half-truths. Although it may be expedient to deceive the workforce about an expected downturn in profits or to try motivating employees with vague promises of bigger bonuses in return for higher productivity, ultimately these strategies backfire. People resent being lied to, no matter what the reason for the lie. Once people realize they have been deceived, they never again work for the deceiver with the same enthusiasm or creativity. A study conducted by International Survey Research in Chicago demonstrates how important the truth is to employees. After seventeen years of studying 2.4 million workers in thirty-two industrial sectors, the researchers found that the number one thing employees really want in the workplace is *to be treated with uncompromising truth.*

Workplace angels meet this request in all sorts of ways. Some tell positive truths routinely: congratulating employees on a recent promotion, recognizing someone's quality work on a project, or just offering appreciation for someone's attitude and enthusiasm. Speaking positive truths every day requires little effort but makes both the truth teller and truth receiver feel terrific.

Other truths are harder to tell. As you learn from some of the stories in this chapter, workplace angels are willing to be straight with people even if what they have to say makes everyone uncomfortable and the news is not good. Some angels even risk their jobs for the truth; they tell a superior that he is doing something wrong, or they go to the media to expose an unethical practice.

Most of the time, however, truth telling is not so dramatic. The workplace angels in this chapter find that their honesty transforms their jobs. They do not feel two-faced or compromised as managers and leaders; they do not go home at night feeling they lead one life at work and another (more ethical) life with the family. They feel they are true to themselves and not wearing a mask for purposes of work. The notion of being oneself in work situations is very important to these angels. For them, truth is not only in the telling but also in the doing. They would feel duplicitous if they were to do anything that violated their values and beliefs.

John Keats's "Ode on a Grecian Urn" ends with these lines:

Beauty is truth, truth beauty
That is all ye know on earth and all ye need to know.

As well as the verse expresses the power of truth for workplace angels, I disagree with Keats in one respect: truth is but one of *seven* things that are "all ye need to know."

It is also important to note that there are both positive and negative truths. Positive truths are easy to share. For many angels, they come naturally. These people do it because "that's how they see it." As one angel stated, "I don't have time to tell half-truths. I feel that if I speak up, and truthfully share the positive things I see in others, I will set a standard in my workplace for others to do the same."

Still other angels have found that positive truth telling leads to an open, more trusting atmosphere where problems are addressed more rapidly. One manager angel put it this way: "I find people in our office much less defensive since we started setting up support networks where workers can gather and candidly share their problems and concerns. Ultimately, we arrive at solution finding—a process we find possible because someone acknowledged the truth."

Fifteen centuries ago, St. Augustine wisely said that faith "is to believe that which you do not see. Truth is to see what you have believed." Workplace angels do both. They believe that a better workplace is available at any time and therefore see signs of this every day.

This chapter is about positive truth telling and the results of that rendering. As you read each story, see how it applies to a workplace in which knowing and speaking the truth can set you free. When sharing of positive truth is ongoing, the foundation of trust is created.

Truth Is Her Motto

Truth is about responding to the urge of spirit within, giving expression to your greatest potential. It is through truth that challenges dissolve into great blessings.

A<small>NNA</small> M<small>C</small>G<small>OVERN</small>, <small>WORKPLACE ANGEL</small>

W hy Chicago?" As she diligently wrote the question in her journal, Anna McGovern knew the answer would come eventually. She also knew that it would probably reveal itself in some unexpected opportunity. She was on a journey, one that had started many years earlier. She had learned to not question why, but to embrace the moment as it was meant to be and learn from it.

She had recently accepted a position with a large plastics manufacturer in the home office. Corporate life was not new to Anna. She had worked for several companies over the past five years, always in an upper-level capacity. She was familiar with the ever-present political pressures of most corporate cultures, but she was able to successfully maintain her own individuality while still following corporate protocol.

Anna was assigned to a high-profile project that would last all summer. The opportunity would become one of her most valuable and enlightening lessons, a lesson in truth.

It all began when Sharon, the project manager, called an emergency meeting. She reported that the project's resources had been cut, meaning that each team member would be expected to work at least a sixty-hour week. This did not include travel time, as the project was off site; in addition, many would be commuting well over an hour's travel in each direction.

Anna could feel the atmosphere in the room change. She sensed frustration, apprehension, and fear. She knew that for many people, these strict time commitments would create great burdens on them as well as their families. She also knew that these feelings were intensified because of the recent cutback in personnel in their department. People were probably feeling lucky they had jobs at all. For these reasons as well as all of their other concerns, they were choosing to hold in their feelings of discontent and be silent.

While Anna was faced with some of the same concerns, she did not share their fear. Her trust in faith allowed her to look beyond the fear objectively to seek the truth in the situation. While the others sat motionless around her, she asked Sharon to explain what exactly they would be doing that required so much of their time. She felt that this was a reasonable question and one that all of them deserved to have answered. In a series of short, blunt statements, Sharon told the team to do it her way "because she said so." Anna noticed Sharon's total lack of clarity and detail in her answers. She wondered if Sharon was purposely trying to be deceptive or if her insecurities were masked as ego.

Continuing to seek the truth, Anna decided to ask the same question again. Some of the listeners might have thought it to be a courageous move, since Sharon had clearly established her role as the authority and decision maker on the project. Some probably believed, as Anna did, that a true leader leads with clarity and truth, not with a big stick and empty words. So, while the others continued sitting in the shadows, Anna calmly raised her hand and asked the same question: "What exactly will we be doing that takes sixty hours a week to accomplish?"

This time Sharon did not even try to cushion her response. It was obvious to Anna that she was angry, and the anger was definitely focused on her. Once again Anna called upon her faith, trusting she would be able to meet Sharon's angry resolve with truth and the clarity that would come from it.

Sharon grew even angrier when she saw that her attempt to break Anna's spirit through intimidation was not working. She also appeared very uncomfortable with Anna's attempt to bring her to truth.

Anna held her ground, and although the question still remained open and unresolved, the meeting went forward as planned. Sharon's conduct suggested that rather than lose face anymore with the team, she would feel safer addressing the matter one-on-one, outside of the group. She labeled Anna as a trouble maker, someone who was uncooperative and obviously there to undermine her efforts and make her look bad. Anna used this time to work through her own process of understanding. She stepped back so she could look forward. She knew she would be back.

Immediately following their meeting, Sharon confronted Anna. She was unaccustomed to having her authority questioned. This behavior was just politically incorrect; it just was not done. Anna tried to explain that she had no problem with working the hours if they were necessary for the good of the project; she just needed some clarity on the process. Could they possibly approach it from a different angle? Could Sharon explain the process, or even give her some reading material that would account for the long hours?

Anna also tried to explain that she had established balance in her life, and that it was necessary to her well-being. If she were expected to work at her best level of competency, she would need to keep this balance. Sharon looked totally flustered at this point and said she would have to get back to her on the matter.

Sharon then elevated the discussion to the person to whom Anna reported directly and to human resources. Anna was given a chance to give her side of the story as well. HR had heard rumblings around the office concerning abusive, invasive conditions on the project, as well as on others that Sharon had been involved in. They could not take any action unless someone would come forward and report it.

Anna was glad to be given a chance to explain her actions. She called on God, as she often did, to "give her the words" as she began to recount to the HR representatives the details surrounding this incident—that is, to tell the truth. The HR people were disturbed by what they heard. An investigation was launched immediately following Anna's report. Sharon was told that she could not force people to work such hours without offering proper justification. If the job was not getting done because of a problem that seemed performance-related, then they could deal with the situation as it arose. They made it clear that she would be held accountable continuously, throughout the life of this and her other projects, for the use of people's time.

The project lasted three months. There were many obstacles along the way, but it was a huge success overall. Anna met these obstacles in the same fashion she had met others; she looked at them as opportunities—life's little learning lessons. Her optimism, good humor, and sense of well-being were contagious. By opening the door to truth early on in the game, she had set a path for truth to grow and prosper. The others were able to take advantage of this freedom as well. When I asked Anna for her definition of truth, she said simply, "Truth is about responding to the urge of spirit within, giving expression to your greatest potential. It is through truth that challenges dissolve into great blessings."

--------- ANGEL REFLECTIONS AND ACTIONS ---------

Reflection What truth would you tell if you had the faith or courage to do so?

Action Write down the truths you would tell if you had the faith and courage to do so, and for a week take time each morning to pray that they be revealed in your workplace. A number of workplace angels have tried this and found that God has a way of revealing these truths.

Fifteen Years of Healing

Through various exercises designed to show the benefit of cooperative teamwork through truth sharing, the awareness started to dawn on a few of the more cynical employees that continued conflict was hurting everyone in the plant.

BILL DEFOORE, *WORKPLACE ANGEL*

When Bill DeFoore was called in to assist in a truth-sharing session, he was not prepared for the outcome. Here, in Bill's own words, is an angel experience that illustrates belief in truth in the workplace.

WE WERE FINISHING our breakfast and having coffee, about to begin a three-day course on self-awareness, communication training, and conflict resolution. I was one of the instructors for the course.

The air in the room was heavy. No one was smiling. The cliques of the opposing groups were evident. Fear and animosity were palpable in the atmosphere that surrounded hushed conversations in the comfortable turn-of-the-century bed-and-breakfast-style hotel meeting room.

The scene was a gathering of forty-five employees caught up in a violent struggle between management and union members in a manufacturing plant. There were recent death threats against the plant manager and his family. Union-led strikes had been recurring for fifteen years, with no lasting resolution. At the time of the meeting, no contract for wages and other terms of employment was in effect; workers were operating under a management-enforced contract. Neither side held any level of trust in the other. Over the years, conflicts in the plant had reached proportions that drew media attention and made headlines in the local newspaper.

Union members were convinced that management did not care about their needs and was only interested in profit at the expense of the people working in the plant. Management saw the union members as aggressive, obstinate, and unwilling to compromise. Participation in the training was voluntary, and those who came had done so skeptically, with little hope of positive outcome. Just showing up was a significant act of trust on the part of everyone there. In the room were laborers, maintenance staff, supervisors, and management, sitting together in a large circle. This had never happened before. To the quiet amazement of many in the room, the plant manager was also present. Having done many trainings of this sort, I found this man's commitment to be exceptional among his peers. He was not only present but participated in every aspect of the training along with all of the other employees, without dominating or taking a leadership position.

On the first day the training was informative, light, and fun, with music, skits, and lots of small-group activities. As we moved into the second day, the atmosphere started to warm up, as participants began to realize that this material could be useful to them in improving their personal and family lives as well as the quality of their work experience. Through various exercises designed to show the benefit of cooperative teamwork through truth sharing, the awareness started to dawn on a few of the more cynical employees that continued conflict was hurting everyone in the plant. Some began to understand that shared vision and a spirit of cooperation would be to the benefit of every employee, their families, and the company itself.

But this was simply not enough. A positive group experience and new intellectual understanding were not powerful or pervasive enough to penetrate the walls of anger, fear, and pain that had separated these people from each other for so long. I found myself thinking of family feuds where people who knew each other all too well managed to sustain violent conflict for generations. We needed no less than a miracle to change the tide of tension and hostility that pervaded this community. We needed an angel, or ideally two or three angels, to emerge from the group. That is exactly what happened.

We finished our lunch break on the second day. I presented an exercise designed to allow participants to express their feelings in a safe and structured manner, with no retribution. The unspoken goal was to establish trust in relationships where there had been none, through a process of truth telling.

With five managers present, the participants were invited to speak to them regarding whatever issues they considered most important. The structure was for the speaker to say how he felt about a particular event or circumstance, using "I" statements. The focus was initially on feelings of anger, fear, and sadness, followed by expression of more positive feelings. The first segment was to remove barriers to accessing the good intentions we believed everyone maintained beneath the surface. The listener was simply to repeat what the speaker had said and ask if it were a correct reflection of the speaker's words.

Samuel, a union steward, was one of the first to speak. As he walked slowly across the room, I sensed the significance of his actions. Everyone's eyes were riveted on him. He walked straight to the chair across from Michael, the plant manager. Though his voice was trembling, Samuel relied on the structure of the exercise to express his sadness to the plant manager. There was no question he was genuine. I felt that he had never talked this way in his entire life. There was electricity in the room as he began.

"I'm very sad for what you and your family have gone through since last August," Samuel said, speaking slowly to get all the words right. The plant manager was so moved that he did not respond for a few moments, during which he fought back tears. In the silence, everyone in the room felt the pain he had gone through, especially the late-night phone calls sending fear into the hearts of the people he loved most. Compassion flowed through Samuel into Michael, from all of us watching.

"Samuel," he replied at last, "I hear you saying that you feel very sad for what my family and I have been through since last August. Is that correct?" Samuel nodded, they shook hands, and the union leader returned to his seat.

No one had thought Samuel would do what he did. He acted in spite of years of cynicism, anger, and pessimism and took a risk on behalf of compassion and caring. Though his angel wings were invisible, this tough, work-hardened man showed who he truly was through this graceful, love-filled act. As a union leader respected by his fellow members, he was the only person in the room who could have exerted that kind of impact. He did not know the power of his choice; he simply acted from his heart. This is how he invited the angel within him to enter the room, and through truth telling to enter the hearts and minds of all of us there with him.

The exchange of these two men opened the flood gates to all of the unexpressed emotion from years gone by. Anger, fear, and sorrow were expressed openly and abundantly by almost everyone in the group. The other instructor and I coached them on staying within the guidelines we had set up for the communication process. The structure was essential to providing a safe container for the powerful emotions that these people so desperately needed to express. Slowly, as the hours passed, the magical and elusive spirit we call "trust" began to pervade the room through truth telling. There was squirming, throat clearing, sniffing, and nose blowing all around. Many of these men and women had known each other and worked side by side for as long as thirty years; anyone with less than ten years on the job was considered a newcomer.

Slowly, it dawned on me that all along there had been a profound and caring connection among these people. The unexpressed fear, conflict, and hostility were simply blocking these deeper, more compassionate feelings. As I reflected on these ideas, it did not occur to me that another angel was about to emerge.

Michael didn't know what hit him. As plant manager, he always intended to do the right thing, and yet he often did exactly the wrong thing. Most of the time, he simply did not know what else to do. After the participants who chose to speak had expressed their feelings, it was time for the members of management to express their feelings to the group. Standing slowly, as if he were afraid he might fall, Michael said in a shaky voice, "I believe we can get past some of these problems that have been holding us back, and create something fantastic together. I really want each and every one of you to enjoy your job and feel that this is a great place to work." I could tell that this sounded like more management mumbo-jumbo to many of the workers, although he was genuinely trying to break out of some old patterns.

But Michael shocked us all with what he did next. Most managers we had previously worked with spoke with one or two employees in this phase of the process, but this man spoke to every participant in the room. Most impressive of all, he made very personal and moving comments to each individual he addressed.

Placing his chair in front of Samuel. Michael expressed feelings that showed he had always had a personal interest in this man, even though Samuel was in the "opposing camp": "I've watched you, Samuel, and I've always been impressed with the leadership you show with your coworkers. It's not something you do, necessarily, it's more about who you are." As Michael spoke these words, there were poorly concealed looks of amazement on the faces of the other union members. This was an incredible breakthrough! The two men had silently respected each other for years, and for the first time they were able to show how they felt in a way that allowed them to maintain their dignity.

Michael's wings began to unfold as we watched him move around the room and place his chair in front of every single person in the group. In his words and manner, he demonstrated that he had been silently and steadily paying attention to each of these people for many years, and that he felt responsible for their welfare. He told stories of interactions that some of them did not recall, though he did. The looks on the faces of some of the lower-paid workers as Michael spoke personally and truthfully with them were beyond value. They were simultaneously shocked, touched, and impressed with his knowledge of them and his attention to their individual jobs and families. Some of them had no idea he even knew their names.

Though I had known most of these people only a few weeks, and some only for two days, my heart was overflowing and tears were in my eyes as I watched them bridge the gaps and take down the walls that had kept them apart for so long.

We moved toward the end of the training and began our wrap-up, in which each person had an opportunity to say some final words about what he or she had learned and experienced in the three days together. There was much laughter and joking, as long-withheld feelings of relief and optimism slowly emerged to fill the gaps left by dispelled fear and anger.

As with any change process, some people were still withholding their willingness to trust. A few made sober and sincere comments about wanting to "wait and see" how this carried over to the workplace. There were many statements from participants who were amazed by what had occurred and still couldn't believe it. The predominant mood was relaxed and optimistic, however, and one woman, tears streaming down her cheeks, summed up the experience for many of us in well-chosen words: "What I have seen here is a miracle. I have seen fifteen years of healing take place in this room. I never thought it would happen." We all sat quietly in the silence that followed, experiencing the tremendous power of truth to create trust.

——————— ANGEL REFLECTIONS AND ACTIONS ———————

Reflection How can you share truths more frequently to build trust?

Action Initiate a series of truth-telling sessions in which you share positive truths for the first four or five meetings. Once you have established trust, bring in truths that are still positive but point to some work that must be carried out (such as those Bill DeFoore describes).

Truth Above All Else

He came to see that by first finding the truth about who he was, he would then be better able to share himself more completely, and through his sharing he would find his purpose and ultimately his joy.

SUSAN FIGNAR, *WORKPLACE ANGEL OF TRUTH*

As Galileo once stated, "All truths are easy to understand once they are discovered; the point is to discover them." Susan Fignar is an expert at discovering truths. As a specialist in the area of image consulting, she focuses on internal development as the key to developing a successful professional presence.

According to Susan, to be in truth is to be truthful first to ourselves. She coaches individuals to get to "know who they are." She points out that a lot of people who exhibit impatience or are unapproachable have difficulty with this. In their attempt to avoid rejection and their need to be perfect, they in fact alienate people. People have to trust that by being vulnerable with others they create a safe space for others to share their own vulnerabilities. She says, "I work with many executives who have trouble being truthful about their weaknesses. They are fearful that they might lose their jobs if they share in this way with others. They think that to admit a weakness here or there is to admit you can't do the whole job."

In her one-on-one coaching, Susan instructs people in how to show their vulnerabilities—elements of their true selves that heighten their awareness and trust that they are wonderful human beings. They have to be willing to share these parts of their true selves with others: "How you look, act, and feel are the three key elements of image. A lot of people have one or two. Not many have all three. We all have to work on this." Through her coaching, people learn to see that it is safe to share vulnerabilities to trust her process that leads to truth.

Through her coaching, people undertake a journey to truth wherein they face their fears and end up being able to lead others on the same journey.

Susan offers a recent example to show how she works with others to share their truth. An executive we will call John was sent to her in an effort to save him from possible firing since his current management style would not make the transition well in his company's change initiatives, which were creating a new work environment. Given an ultimatum to work with Susan or look elsewhere for a position, he called her.

During their first session, Susan recalls just listening to his view of what he thought was happening in his workplace. She was truthful with him when she shared that he appeared un-approachable. Perhaps because he was close to being let go from his current organization, he seemed open to her advice. Susan recommended he think about how he showed himself to others; what were his conversations like? She even recom-mended that he change his voice mail message to sound friendlier and more positive. She also offered her perception that John seemed closed and aloof.

John took back his first homework assignment: among other things, to journal his interactions for one week. Through his journaling process, he saw that he held back his feelings even from himself. He realized that to build trusting relation-ships with others he needed to be more revealing and truthful about his feelings, first to himself and then to others. When he met with Susan again, she saw visible signs of change. First, rather than frowning, when he met her he smiled. He an-nounced he had something very exciting to tell her: "I changed my voice mail message, as we discussed, so that it shares more of my feelings and wishes for them to come to me with any problems and then to have a 'most pleasant day.' Within the day, people started coming up to me and asking me what was going on. They wanted to know what was different about me.

They smiled during our conversation, and then they left with what seemed like a lighter spring in their step."

Susan continued to coach John, who still works for the company today. He came to see that by first finding the truth about who he was, he would then be better able to share himself more completely, and through his truth sharing he would find his purpose and ultimately his joy. He was validated for his truth many times over by his colleagues and family members.

——————— ANGEL REFLECTIONS AND ACTIONS ———————

Reflection What is your truth about "the way you show up" in the eyes of those in your workplace?

Reflection What can you do more of, or do differently, today to be as you want others to perceive you?

Action Find a friend who can share in truth with you how you "show up." I have used Susan Fignar's coaching techniques and find that most of the time we are not aware of how we truly look to others. Working with a friend in a safe space develops your truths, which brings about the results you might have found elusive up to now.

The Truth Teller

I was aware of the needs of the department and was always on the lookout for highly competent people. When I found competent people, I wrote a job description around their attributes.

KAROL EMMERICK, *WORKPLACE ANGEL*

It has been five years since Karol Emmerick left full-time corporate America, where she was vice president, treasurer, and chief accounting officer of the $20 billion Dayton Hudson Corporation. Having climbed the corporate ladder for twenty-one years, she found herself one of Dayton Hudson's top ten corporate officers in 1989. At that time, with forty people working for her, she was responsible for managing the corporation's financing, investments, financial planning, and accounting and reporting.

Throughout her time at Dayton Hudson, Karol wove her wisdom and truth throughout the organization to influence positive change. "Everyone has gifts," she says. "I could never hire a person to fit a specific job description, because I felt I could never put an individual in a box. I was aware of the needs of the department and was always on the lookout for highly competent people. When I found competent people, I wrote a job description around their attributes." Her strategies were very successful, resulting in increased employee productivity and revenues as well as lower employee turnover. Before all else, she looked for what would be best for each person in the department. In operating this way, she found that doing right by the person she did right for the corporation.

For example, if an employee needed to spend more time with the family, Karol didn't try to talk the person out of working part-time. She was willing to take the best of what each person could give her.

Telling the truth has always put her at the threshold of opportunities and conflict. In the early 1980s, she started an internal women's network. The first thing she noticed was that low-level and nonexempt employees had little access if any to training that would grow them into higher-level positions. There were no opportunities for, say, leadership training. As president of the network, she found ways to provide opportunities for these people to practice and develop leadership skills. She also went to management and persuaded them that all employees deserved to be developed. Her championing of such causes brought about new program tracks for employees.

Karol was known as an encourager and advocate. Managers knew they could count n her to tell the truth; what she said came from her heart as much as her head. They also knew she would take the time to listen to the individual needs of employees and, as much as possible, become their personal champion. As she puts it, "I always looked at these people as precious human beings. I have seen others who treat people differently. I knew that by taking time with people—and that might mean an incredible amount of time—I gave them the tools to enable themselves to be the best they could be. This helped all of us realize tremendous gains."

Karol found herself becoming an excellent judge of character. Her motto was "grow or go," which was meant as a pact between herself and employees. "This was a form of tough love through truth telling. I upheld this motto because I cared about them and their success, and it worked. There was one woman with whom I worked who was a great employee, but she was so shy. I required her to go to assertiveness training, from which she benefited greatly."

Karol's truth comes out as frankness combined with creativity. As she sees it, it has enabled her to nurture many along the way. Today she works pro bono as a consultant to individuals and organizations on issues related to philanthropy, volunteerism, governance, women, work, and faith. She serves on the boards of Piper Funds and Slumberland and is an executive fellow at the University of St. Thomas Graduate School of Business. She also serves on numerous nonprofit boards. In the last year alone, she offered her talents gratis on twenty-one weekends.

Her two passions in life are encouraging people in their giving of time, talent, and treasure to God's Kingdom and serving as the steward of a beautiful hilltop garden she and her husband have created.

How to build an environment of truth in your workplace? Karol recommends you find people who will tell you the truth but do so because they care. She has two main talks she likes to give. "What's Worth the Rest of Your Life?" focuses on working from your gifts and passion and looking at your life as an investment: "Your goal is to figure out what God meant for you to do with your life. Don't waste it!" The other talk is "Why I Left at the Top," her personal story of how she brought a world of truth to the world of work.

――――― ANGEL REFLECTIONS AND ACTIONS ―――――

Reflection Who can you serve today by telling them their truths to help them become the best workers they can be?

Action Share *your* truth with someone in your workplace. The truth is we are all teachers and students at different times. If you look at this truth, you see that anyone at any age is a great partner with whom you can share knowledge, and in that sharing accelerate your career and your well-being. Partnering in the workplace is the ultimate in partnering or alliance building. Your colleagues, your associates, and your employees become your partners in growth. You are saying, "We're here for each other." As one good manager told me, "I work for my employees. They don't work for me."

Truth and Honest Abe

The greatest homage we can pay to truth is to use it.

—RALPH WALDO EMERSON

At the Thai Town Restaurant in Streamwood, Illinois, there is a very special bronze statue of President Abraham Lincoln, measuring ten inches tall, a replica of the Lincoln Memorial in Washington, D.C. At this restaurant is an even more special owner, named Iam Thamasucharit, whose very foundation for living is based on truth.

Iam's Thai restaurant, besides having outstanding food, offers patrons the opportunity to pay back a leader in our American history who gave so much to his country. The statue of Lincoln has become a place for people to leave their spare change—money that Iam makes sure is given back to the great past president, whose tomb is in the state capital in Springfield.

It happened one day as two customers at the cash register paid for their meal. One noticed that his friend had some spare change, pointed to the bronze statue, and asked, "Why don't you leave your change at the feet of President Lincoln? You know, if you rub his head and make a wish, it's good luck!"

At his friend's suggestion, the customer put his coins at Lincoln's feet and then rubbed the bronze head. Iam found this behavior quite curious, but he thought, *If this is what others do with Mr. Lincoln, then I will not interfere.*

Soon customer after customer was leaving spare change for Mr. Lincoln. Eventually, the spare change started flowing over the bottom ledge of the statue, spilling onto the floor. Because Iam was convinced this was not his money, he assured anyone who asked, "This is Mr. Lincoln's money." He saw he had to find a way to get the money over to Mr. Lincoln.

Eventually he was referred to the Illinois preservation agency that maintains Lincoln's tomb. When the agency receptionist answered the phone, she was greeted by a man who requested to know where he could send money that was "Mr. Lincoln's." At first the receptionist thought someone was playing a rather crude practical joke. Eventually, through Iam's broken English, she was able to understand his request. She gave him the address of the agency, and Iam immediately wrote a check to cover the exact amount of the coins he had gathered so diligently.

To this day, he continues to gather spare change for President Lincoln. It has amounted to more than four hundred dollars in the last four years.

An additional, interesting note to this story is that about a year ago a group of people came into Iam's restaurant. When he came to their table to take their order, one man in the group asked, "Hey, what do you do with all that change sitting by the bronze statue of President Lincoln at your front counter?" When Iam explained, the man smiled excitedly: "I can't believe it! So you're the guy who has been sending that money to us in Springfield! I work with the Illinois Historic Preservation Agency!" Iam beamed with pride, for he knew he had done what he felt was the only right thing to do for a country and a person who had given him the opportunity to speak and live in truth.

Iam's commitment to truth is about behaving congruently with his principles. In other words, he walks his talk, giving back to those he feels have given him the greatest opportunity of all: freedom.

——— ANGEL REFLECTIONS AND ACTIONS ———

Reflection Who personifies truth for you, and how can you follow his or her example?

Action Gather ideas from coworkers to help generate an atmosphere of truth throughout your workplace. One large pharmaceutical company started a bulletin board filled with quotes and stories on the subject of truth. The best stories were then used in newsletters to its thousands of customers and placed on its Website. The organization posted record earnings that quarter. At its annual retreat, the originators of the idea were honored and given an award the company called the "Truth in Action" award. It has now become an annual honor for employees who come up with programs and processes that help the company grow in its belief in truth.

She Writes the Truth and Sets Them Free

Living in truth means living in harmony with yourself.

LINDSEY NOVAK, *WORKPLACE ANGEL*

One of Lindsey Novak's workplaces is the *Chicago Tribune,* where she has been delivering belief in truth to millions of readers every week for the past six years. Her syndicated advice column, "At Work," focuses on sensitive issues and workplace problems ranging from dysfunctional bosses and difficult coworkers to office gossip and sexual harassment. Of course, she also makes room for practical tips and strategies for getting ahead in the workplace without stepping on others in the process. For Lindsey, belief in truth is a permanent fabric woven seamlessly through her weekly columns. She makes reference to one of her favorite poems as a guidepost for how she lives her life and shares her truth every day with others:

There is a destiny that makes us brothers.
None goes this way alone.
All that we send into the lives of others
Comes back into our own.

—ANONYMOUS

The poem shows her that if you are true to others you are true to yourself: "Living in truth means living in harmony with yourself, and if you are in harmony with yourself you wouldn't think of hurting someone else. In fact, as you grow more truthful with yourself, you start to recognize more that everyone has different gifts that *complement* rather than *compete* with others." She goes on: "This process of becoming more truthful with yourself first is the foundation of great teamwork. I hear from many people, however, who work at companies where they are on assigned teams but instead of working as a team are actually in competition with one another."

Lindsey emphasizes that the problem lies in looking enviously at others' talents rather than seeing that each person has something unique and complementary to offer. She has seen that jealousy comes out of insecurity, out of not valuing oneself. In her column she offers a way for people to live positively and shine in the workplace without blinding others. Her basic philosophy is that "people cheat themselves by not appreciating their own God-given talents. They cheat themselves of becoming truly successful, contented, and prosperous human beings by feeling they have to compete and crush others to get ahead. The same underlying anger can also hurt employees when they turn it into dishonesty against their companies."

In a recent column on job dishonesty, the headline read, "Is On-the-Job Dishonesty Ever Justified?" She writes: "First of all, honesty is not old-fashioned. Morals, ethics, and values are bred into many children so they will grow up to be valuable individuals who contribute to society. Unfortunately, some parents don't impart these values, so children grow up selfish, self-centered, and self-absorbed, which can lead to dishonesty."

Lindsey was responding to a reader's question regarding personal responsibility in the workplace. The reader said she believed most employees are not honest, committing acts ranging from taking home paper clips to arriving late, stealing company time by leaving early, taking long lunches and breaks, and making too many personal phone calls.

Lindsey believes the truth is that employees do these things just to "even the score" in the workplace. Although she recognizes that some companies are very supportive of their employees—treating people with respect and recognizing their hard work through both monetary and nonmonetary ways—other companies are cutting back on benefits and in general making life miserable for even their long-time, high-salaried employees.

Echoing what we suggested in the opening of this chapter, Lindsey says: "People simply want employers to respect them and the jobs they do. They are willing to put in a hard day's work if they receive positive feedback regarding their performance. When people no longer like their jobs, their bosses, or their companies, but it's the only job available at the time, they have no choice but to stay. So they do what they can to make it tolerable—maybe even enjoyable. And sometimes that involves being dishonest."

The thousands of letters she has received from workers reveal workplaces riddled with pain. Her view is that most workers are honest, hardworking people who want to feel they are needed, that what they have to offer is highly valued. She believes that given the right environment of truth and caring, any workplace can be one in which workers respect one another, their employers, their customers, and most of all themselves.

——————— ANGEL REFLECTIONS AND ACTIONS ———————

Reflection What one thing can you do today to honor your employer?

Action Create an employee amnesty day. One organization created such a day to address acts of employee dishonesty in the workplace. Employees were asked to change just one thing they were doing in the workplace that they might consider dishonest; in return, all employees would receive two extra vacation days for the year. They were asked to submit a statement of the act of dishonesty they would now change (on typed, folded sheets of paper input anonymously through departmental amnesty boxes), and a list was compiled, sent to all employees, and posted in the employee lunchroom. Within three months, the organization experienced a 50 percent decrease in stolen office supplies and a 67 percent decrease in employee absenteeism.

Angel Advice Corner

Bringing More Truth into Your Workplace

Here are some simple tips for bringing more truth into your workplace. Review them regularly for further direction in building the power of truth in your world of work.

- *See and hear the truth of children.* They are not yet filled with the hatred of prejudice nor the fear of rejection. They are filled with basic truths, if only we listen—truths that provide profound direction in our busy worlds.

- *Zealously seek the truth.* The real wealth in the world is in our willingness to constantly seek the truth.

- *Listen with your eyes to see the truth about others.* People either confirm or deny their statements with their actions.

- *Avoidance of self creates chaos.* Do not hide from your truths, no matter how painful they may feel at first. Change the things that you do not believe help you grow, one small step at a time.

- *When speaking negative truths, remember to focus on the performance rather than the performer.* The next time you make an assumption about someone in your workplace, ask yourself, "Am I criticizing the performer or the performance?" Telling negative truth about another is criticizing only the performance. For our workplaces to be a source of healing, we need to focus on the performance, not the performer. In this way, we can still support the person while realizing that we all make mistakes.

- *Limit your time for complaining.* One angel manager describes a technique for truth telling. She allows fifteen minutes for complaints, followed by fifteen minutes of solutions. Her employees know well her reasons for this approach, since she makes it clear she believes that time spent truthfully addressing problems (but only limited time) satisfies the need to address issues without getting emotionally entangled in them. On the other hand, the fifteen minutes for solutions allows time for breaking through to more productive actions and thoughts. Her results speak for themselves. From employee satisfaction surveys, daily comments, and marked productivity increases, it is apparent that her process of getting the "truth of each matter" has brought about great rewards.

- *Understand the gray area between truths.* I always say that when two truths are presented by two people, the real truth lies somewhere in between. This allows a gray area to exist that enables both parties room for flexibility. Rather than saying, "I'm right, you're wrong," you might say, "It doesn't matter who is right; I want to work this out so we're both satisfied with the outcome."

- *Guide others with the truth.* I once asked my son Graham if my husband and I were different from other parents. He responded: "Yes. Other parents manage their children. You guide us with the truth." Think about how you might play the role of workplace angel, guiding others with the truth.

Truth: A Summary of Angel Actions

Write the truths you would tell if you had the faith and courage to do so, and for a week take time each morning to pray that they be revealed in your workplace.

Initiate a series of truth-telling sessions in which you share positive truths for the first four or five meetings. Once you have established trust, bring in truths that are still positive but point to some work that must be carried out.

Find a friend who can share in truth with you how you "show up." Working with a friend in a safe space develops your truths, which brings about the results you might have found elusive up to now.

Share *your* truth with someone in your workplace. Because we are all teachers and students at different times, anyone at any age is a great partner with whom you can share knowledge, and in that sharing accelerate your career and your well-being. Partnering in the workplace is the ultimate in partnering or alliance. Your colleagues, your associates, and your employees become your partners in growth.

Gather ideas from coworkers to help generate an atmosphere of truth throughout your workplace. Recall the example of a pharmaceutical company's bulletin board of quotes and stories on the subject of truth, display of the best story in customer newsletters and a Website, and an annual "Truth in Action" award for employees whose ideas for programs and processes help the company grow in its belief in truth.

Create an employee amnesty day, to address acts of employee dishonesty in the workplace. Using a system of gathering comments that ensures anonymity, ask employees to change just one thing they are doing in the workplace that they might consider dishonest; in return, employees receive appropriate rewards, such as extra vacation days for the year.

TRUST

Being Open and Vulnerable with Confidence

I think we may safely trust a good deal more than we do. We may waive just so much care of ourselves as we honestly bestow elsewhere.

—HENRY DAVID THOREAU

Trust in the workplace is a very serious issue. Tom Peters maintains that for organizations "adding trust is the issue of the decade." Perhaps never before, since the beginning of the Industrial Revolution, have there been so many trust issues in the workplace. Whether it is employers seeking loyal employees or employees seeking trustworthy employers, trust issues abound.

Many organizations are frantically searching for ways to build employee morale, using outside consultants and speakers to motivate through developing team building, customer service, and leadership. They also bring in experts to conduct employee morale and trust surveys. Yet the same organizations often fail to address the concerns that show up in these surveys. Instead, management spends 80 percent of its time identifying problems and only 20 percent of the time doing anything about them.

However, those organizations and employees who have taken it upon themselves to build trust through long-term initiatives in the workplace are receiving great benefits. The stories in this section showcase how others have developed this belief, which brings about great improvements in the quality of daily work life.

Most if not all of the seven beliefs of workplace angels involve belief in trust. Faith (Chapter One) is often synonymous with trust in the context of angel beliefs. Whereas faith represents trust in the divine, trust focuses on belief in a person or thing. Additionally, hope is also often used to define trust. Certainly, courage evolves from trusting that even though fear is present, the desired outcome will be achieved, or that the choice you make is right no matter what the outcome. Further, when trust is intertwined with truth, you trust that the decision you make or the words you speak are based on truth. Finally, love emanates from deep-seated trust that you are leading from your heart rather than your head.

To undervalue the power of trust is therefore to limit its contribution in creating a new world of work. By building your relationships on a foundation of trust, you come to experience the other seven beliefs and the powerful gifts they return to you.

The workplace angels in this chapter know how essential this belief is in almost every aspect of daily work. They have experienced firsthand how lack of trust can tear an organization apart. They also know trust must be developed daily to remain an effective tool for personal as well as organizational growth.

Building Trust Where the Sky Is the Limit

Trust is the basic ingredient for any relationship to continue indefinitely. Trusting relationships are the only ones that really count.

DAN DICKINSON, WORKPLACE ANGEL OF TRUST

Twenty years ago, Dan Dickinson was the president of a $50 million used aircraft sales company. He was building relationships internationally at a time when no one else thought of such a unique way to build business. Today, many of the people in those relationships are friends of a man they have come to respect both in and out of the workplace.

The core business of General Aviation Services is sales, brokerage, and acquisition of turbine and jet aircraft, which sell individually for $500,000 to $5 million. In 1997, sales were over $35 million in turbine aircraft alone. Today, after building hundreds of relationships grounded in trust, Dan and his team have created eight separate businesses. But none of this success is as important as his ability to serve others through the medium of trust building. His attitude is, "I have preexisting relationships around the world; I can exchange opportunities with these people by building trust with them. I can be their connection in the States, and they can be my connection in their respective countries."

Chuck Cooper, vice president at the headquarters in Lake Zurich, Illinois, says that "Dan is so good at developing relationships we have built a tremendously wide variety of alliances. We had a client company come to us recently that would like us to buy them out. They came to trust us, knowing that Dan is fair. He is the kind of person they would like to partner with. I've known Dan for fifteen years and have been working for him for nine years."

At one time, Chuck and Dan were competitors. Chuck was out looking for a job and was referred to Dan by a mutual friend. He knew Dan's great reputation for trustworthiness—for being a team player—although he did not know him personally. "Dan was one of the few people in the industry with a good reputation," he says. "He realized that it was people who really mattered, and that included everyone he came in contact with." Offered an opportunity to interview with Dan, Chuck jumped: "Dan is the kind of employer who allows you to grow. I've never seen someone so good at developing one's strengths while simultaneously compensating for their weaknesses."

Chuck started in aircraft sales but less than four years later was promoted to vice president and sales manager. Dan was also instrumental in starting and building the National Aircraft Resale Association (NARA), with the specific mission of establishing a code of ethics and increasing the confidence of potential buyers. Dan was NARA's second president, serving for two years, and was later chairman.

Another secret element Chuck talks about is Dan's commitment to building trust by going the extra mile. For example, when a young man in the aviation field needed to start his own business, Dan lent him the money and provided him with a start-up inventory on consignment.

Dan's belief in trust offers the broadest opportunity to excel. There are no doors in his office, nor locks on drawers. Dan emphasizes, "An 'in-the-box' thinker would have a very difficult time operating in this environment, since it's permeated with trust."

Dan attributes his core values to his parents. It only seems natural to him to "lay down all the cards at the beginning," as he calls it. "Every relationship I have represents a circle. I look to see if and where our circles of commonality—beliefs, interests, etc.—overlap. Because our transactions are so large and I'm impatient, I believe we should get to the bottom line quickly." This is evident in most of Dan's deals, which he secures with a handshake and later with a simple contract.

"Trust is the basic ingredient for any relationship to continue indefinitely," he says. "Trusting relationships are the only ones that really count." Dan is in good company. His beliefs echo those of Henry Stinson, the American secretary of war during World War II, who said, "The chief lesson I have learned is that the only way to make a man trustworthy is to trust him."

──────── ANGEL REFLECTIONS AND ACTIONS ────────

Reflection Who can you start trusting today to build a relationship of trust?

Action Build trust by finding people with similar values. Whereas your interests change continually, your values tend to remain fairly constant. You will find that special angel alliances with individuals who hold similar values help you become a better person and leader. Write your three most important values or beliefs. How does trust relate to them? For example, suppose your first value is excellence; trust in yourself and others is essential to achieving above-average results.

Building a Place for Trust

Trust is a prerequisite to true innovation and creativity.

Eileen McDargh, *WORKPLACE ANGEL*

Eileen McDargh specializes in creating safe places for people. Depending on the assignment, she could be asked to present a motivational speech or facilitate an executive retreat. What makes her unique, however, is how she does her work. As she puts it, "I spend a great deal of time asking questions of both management and staff, and then I pick out the threads of conversations that create the fabric of the issues the organization is facing."

With more than twenty years of experience, Eileen has found that how people are treated determines their level of trust. She has seen firsthand that when people are in a place where their feelings can be heard and appreciated, they open up to opportunities rather than formulate complaints. She asks questions such as, "How would you like your organization to be when it grows up?" She has found this to be a particularly revealing question because it recognizes that corporations are just like people, always in process; even though some might be considered "ancient," they are still evolving.

What separates her from many advisors is her effort to hold her clients responsible. One organization called to hire her as a motivational speaker. As she has learned, this request often comes packaged with underlying problems that need to be addressed first. She told the client she would have to do research before providing them with a proposal for speaking. What she discovered talking to the organization's employees was a pervasive lack of trust. She then told the company that she would not work with them unless they addressed the problem. They agreed. Later, though, she found they were not taking action on their commitment. They kept doing things as they had always done them, refusing to address the changes they needed to make to build a foundation of trust. It was a lesson she did not want to learn twice.

Today, Eileen makes sure she receives a contract, stating specifically what they will do based on the results of any surveys she recommends they perform: "I tell them if they ask questions and seek responses from others, they have to be willing to deal with the results."

"Trust is a prerequisite to true innovation and creativity," she adds. "Nowadays you don't engage people's minds without first engaging their hearts, which is what the best teachers do. When we went to school growing up, we didn't ask, 'What time slot did you get for that class?' We asked, 'What teacher did you get?'" Eileen believes that the best teachers—the ones who drew out the greatest abilities in their students—treated students with respect, listened to their questions, joined them in the learning process, and created an environment in which the students trusted both the content and the process. She sees her role in the corporate world as a healer, holding up a mirror in which participants can view their own ability to generate this kind of environment.

Eileen realizes that when you engage people's hearts you start the important process of building long-lasting trust. Through her facilitation and keynotes, she helps people experience the trust-building process, taking them on a journey of real-life stories that ignite their desire to build a foundation of trust in their workplaces as well as desire to trust their sense of worth and responsibility in the greater world. Her thriving business is a testimony to her success in asking the tough questions that build trust. It is a labor of love, for which she prays daily: "God, please give the words to build an environment to support, nurture, and grow spirit in these workplaces." Her busy schedule shows that God is certainly listening.

──────── ANGEL REFLECTIONS AND ACTIONS ────────

Reflection What statements about your organization's conduct of work would you make if you were trusted by your management or colleagues?

Reflection What do you do daily to show you are someone worthy of trust?

Action Create a code of conduct for your workplace based on trust. Include, for example, such statements as

- Management doesn't play favorites.
- Our opinions are considered.
- We are kept informed about significant matters that have an impact on our company and our work.
- Differences are valued.
- We listen to each other.

A Trustworthy Soul

No virtue is more universally accepted as a test of good character than trustworthiness.

—HARRY EMERSON FOSDICK

For thirty-five years, Bob Mugnaini was employed by a large beverage company. In 1997, he was let go unexpectedly because of downsizing and elimination of his department. If ever there was a time when Bob had to trust—not just have trust but rely on *blind* trust—it was now. Getting over the shock of losing a job he loved, he was confronted with the uncertainty of unemployment. As he put it, "Where do you go after thirty-five years?"

As the special events manager, he oversaw distribution of the company's products for a number of major events in the Chicagoland area. He loved what he did, his job, his bosses, especially the people he worked with, as well as the press and other vendors with whom he swapped stories. His simple philosophy was based on trusting his people to do the job, knowing it would get done.

His trust in humanity was apparent when he approached a park district employee and sold him on the idea of allowing the park district gym to become the home of a basketball tournament for handicapped kids. The idea was accepted and largely successful, bringing kids from all over the area to compete. His company provided the refreshments and small award badges, but Bob wanted—and personally paid for—trophies because he felt the boys and girls deserved even more recognition.

It was also not unusual for him to drop off products late in the evening on his own time. He welcomed the opportunity to further build trusting relationships with the folks in his community. His trust building extended to involving his family's talents when his son Jeff volunteered to participate with his freestyle bike demonstration team in a festival sponsored by his former employer. Additionally, his wife, Mary, and oldest son, Scott, could often be found at various events, pouring sodas for the crowds.

A former fellow employee and protégé recalls the only time he remembers hearing anything negative from Bob was when he threatened to "break my legs if I didn't finish school." To this day, the young man still stays in touch with his long-time mentor. As Bob emphasizes, "It's all about trust. If you let them know you trust them, they will not disappoint you." He trusted in his ability to talk things out, to correct things if a mistake was made. He would say, "Let's figure out how and why this happened and then do it better next time."

Throughout his thirty-five years, which included twenty years of volunteer basketball coaching for fifth through eighth grades, Bob developed trusting relationships in his community that still exist. The friendships he created with his strong belief in trust surely number in the hundreds. Because of his ability to create trust, even though he lost a job he knew he could now turn to those he had served for so many years to help.

Bob also knew he could reach back into his community for support. It was not necessary to have another important corporate job to continue to serve his community. He held a deep trust that wherever he ended up would be where he was meant to serve. So when an opportunity finally came up at a local school, he became a workplace angel as a custodian. As I chatted with Bob about his new position, I heard the same trust and pride in his new employer as he had held for his old one. He was put there to make a difference; therefore, he was in the right place.

Bob is a genuine workplace angel, one we can all learn from. This is not to say that what happened to him was fair; he took his situation and turned it into an opportunity. As he says, "I now know I have no place to go but up!"

Trust is born with openness, vulnerability, and awareness that we cannot go it alone. No one is self-made. We constantly need others to turn our wants and needs into reality. Bob has understood the process of building—and then tapping into the power of—a community of trusted friends.

─────── ANGEL REFLECTIONS AND ACTIONS ───────

Reflection What actions have you taken that inspire an environment of trust in your workplace?

Action Identify someone in your workplace you can turn to as a role model for building trust. In advance of a face-to-face meeting, write the three things that you would most like to learn from the person. Ask to spend just fifteen minutes twice a month talking about these three things. With time, add to your list new ideas about learning to trust, and share them during your meetings. Combining a focused learning process with spending time with someone you admire yields great insight and builds better understanding of your belief in trust.

Trust as a Philosophy of Working

One first has to be trustworthy to gain trust. I take that obli-gation very seriously.

LESLIE MATTISON, *WORKPLACE ANGEL OF TRUST*

For Leslie Mattison, trust is an integral part of daily work life. As a commercial lender for a large bank, she is responsible for acquiring new customers and additional product sales from existing customers. But her main interest is developing trusting relationships, with coworkers and especially with customers.

In the early stages of her business, when Sally received her first line of credit, she was ecstatic. Unable to obtain credit elsewhere, she had been privately funding her business with high-interest credit cards for the past five years, while praying regularly for a better method. She found herself unable to get ahead of her debt.

On the day she received her line of credit (at a much lower interest rate), she realized that money took a far second to the trust she was building with Leslie. Today she still considers their ongoing friendship one of her greatest business assets.

Trust is a two-way street. Leslie trusted Sally's potential, providing a great deal of practical advice for managing business growth. "Before I met her," Sally recalls, "I met with many lenders who focused on my business but not on me. Leslie was the first person who saw how I was an important part of my business. She helped me believe, to trust in my abilities; she could see the vision I was trying to achieve."

Leslie adds, "After nine years in this industry and four years in retail working with all types of customers, I've learned it all starts and ends with me. I represent my organization. I'm the contact my customers have most of the time. Therefore, the only way my customers will continue to maintain a relationship with my bank is if I am a trustworthy person. Also, no customer will share such intimate information like this if they don't trust me. In order to receive that information, I need to be trustworthy; I need to earn that trust."

Leslie's trust created a safe space for Sally to share the intimate details of her business. As a result of their trusting relationship, Sally has attained success she never knew back when she was on her own, without Leslie's support.

Of course, we all risk exposure when we trust. It takes special angels of trust like Leslie to define what should be the norm in our daily business dealings. "For me," she emphasizes, "trust is essential to every relationship, whether it is in the workplace or at home. Just because it might be 9:00 A.M. on a Monday morning doesn't mean we should have a different standard regarding trust. What you practice at home should be what you practice at work. For me, trust is one of those

beliefs—one of those values, that it is essential to pay attention to at all times. One first has to be trustworthy to gain trust. I take that obligation very seriously."

——————— ANGEL REFLECTIONS AND ACTIONS ———————

Reflection What have you done lately to make yourself more trustworthy?

Reflection Who is waiting to be trusted in your workplace? How will you create a safe space for this person to "come out" in trust?

Action Write five things you have done in the last month to build trust in your workplace. Next, write five other things you will do to build trust in the next thirty days. The process of building trust creates more trusting relationships in your life, and subsequently more satisfaction.

Trust and Bringing Up Our Youth

The girls and their families put their trust in us as an organization to help them gain the kinds of positive developmental experiences that will remain with them all through their lives.

BROOKE WISEMAN, *WORKPLACE ANGEL*

Belief in trust plays a major role in Brooke Wiseman's workplace. As executive director of the Girl Scouts of Chicago, she enacts it every day. She tells us: "Trusting yourself and others is important. It is critical if you are in a position of leadership. Leaders must have trust and faith in the people with whom they are working. I find that the majority of people have the ability and desire to do a good job. You then need to trust them to do the right thing. Otherwise, you never accomplish anything if you are constantly worrying about what your workers are doing or how they are carrying out the details of their work."

Brooke's strong belief in trusting that people do their best often results in employees' attaining higher levels of accomplishment than they ever imagined. The same truth extends to working with a volunteer board of directors: "In girl scouting, our actions are guided by our mission statement. It helps everyone involved with the organization maintain a clear focus as to what we stand for and where we are going. You then trust your board members to carry out the mission and fulfill their stewardship responsibilities. You must have faith that they will do the right thing on behalf of the girls we serve and our many constituents."

Brooke also firmly believes that the organization has a duty and obligation to build trust in the young girls who seek scouting as an outlet for development; interpersonal, social, and leadership skills; friendship; and fun. "Essentially," she says, "the girls and their families put their trust in us as an organization to help them gain the kinds of positive developmental experiences that will remain with them all through their lives."

She also emphasizes that scouting fills an important human service role and that her organization takes that responsibility very seriously. Additionally, she points out that girls need strong female role models to emulate. What some may not know, however, is that the organization reaches girls in every sector of the city, including homeless shelters, juvenile detention centers, and after-school programs in some of the most resource-deprived areas.

Founded more than eighty-five years ago, Girl Scouts of the USA today has approximately three million girls between the ages of five and seventeen and is supported by more than five hundred thousand adult volunteers. Peter Drucker, the renowned management guru and supporter of nonprofits, has often said that Girl Scouts is one of the best management organizations in existence today.

Girl Scouts is an all-girl organization whose primary purpose is to help girls living in cities and from diverse backgrounds develop their full potential. Through an informal education process, adult volunteers serve as role models and deliver the Girl Scout program through structured activities in troop or group settings. The program develops skills in good citizenship, positive self-image, leadership, decision making, and resourcefulness. Volunteers are always needed to work directly with girls or indirectly in a variety of other support positions.

Brooke's commitment to building trust in her organization continues to yield results that benefit her employees as well as those whom her organization serves: the young girls looking for guidance. Along with the organization's half-million volunteers, she offers compelling testimony to the power of trust. Think of the number of lives that have been touched by the work of these people. Think of the young women who have benefited from the relationships formed with older women mentors. Finally, think of the workplaces that now house women who were once scouts and who now provide leadership to others.

——————— ANGEL REFLECTIONS AND ACTIONS ———————

Reflection How can you nurture a workplace grounded in belief in trust?

Reflection Who in your life has provided lessons in believing in trust? How can you honor those people for their contribution to your growth?

Action Get involved with an organization like the Girl Scouts. There are many organizations looking for angels in the workplace. Ask your colleagues and friends, "Who do you know who is truly enjoying their volunteer work?" Then go out and volunteer for those organizations. They are the ones that understand what a gift a volunteer is; these are the places where you fully embrace the benefits of being a successful volunteer.

Trust, God, and Life's Curveballs

*Challenges are the training ground from which all great men
and women develop the character to do great things. We need
to trust that through God, all things do work together for our
good.*

ED HEARN, *WORKPLACE ANGEL*

L ook closely at a penny, a nickel, a dime, or a quarter and
you find the words "In God We Trust." Today, former New
York Mets baseball player Ed Hearn is an exceptional embod-
iment of trust. A few years ago, though, his trust was greatly
challenged.

It all started when a serious shoulder injury brought a pre-
mature end to his baseball career. Then, while making the
transition into corporate America, unbelievably Ed was diagnosed with three life-threatening illnesses: kidney failure, sleep
apnea, and a gamma globulin deficiency. In a short period of
time, he went from being a big, strong, highly conditioned ath-
lete to a man too weak to get out of bed without assistance.
His trust further waned as he faced postoperative depression
following his kidney transplant surgery.

How does the human spirit overcome such a physically and
emotionally draining roller-coaster ride through life? This former major league catcher and World Series champion now
lives to share with others his message, which came from deep
trust in God. As an inspirational speaker and author, he tells
his audiences how he has moved from "the penthouse to the
outhouse and back." His courageous story of rebuilding his life,
with the loving help of family and friends and God, is an ongoing affirmation of the power of trust.

Ed refers to his wife and nurse, Tricia, as "the wind beneath
my wings." Prior to his illness, while still playing for the Mets,
he was introduced to her when he chose to spend time with a

teammate at a cystic fibrosis fundraising luncheon. His desire to help put a smile on some of those little faces afflicted with this disease attracted Tricia to his life as an added benefit. He affectionately refers to his wife as an absolute "gift from God." With her help, support, and trust in God, his own trust grew. He felt safe to ask for the help he needed to overcome the many personal and professional struggles that accompanied his illnesses.

Tricia continues to stand by his side as he "keeps on swinging for life's fences." Their three-year-old son, Cody Carter Hearn, gives him an additional reason for living. Ed sees that through life's hardships come gifts to help us keep trusting. Cody is such a gift.

Through his many speeches, Ed offers great insight into living a happy, productive life, insights drawn from his own lessons in trust. He trusts God, seeks him first, and does not worry about tomorrow.

The realization came two years after his kidney transplant, when he realized that God really did have a plan for his life. He says he read from Scripture: ". . . so I was given a thorn in the flesh and three times I begged God to make me well again. Each time He said, 'No, but I am with you; that is all you need. My strength shows up best in weak people.' Now, I am glad to boast about how weak I am. I am glad to be a living demonstration of Christ's power, instead of showing off my own abilities. For when I am weak, then I am strong. The less I have, the more I depend on Him."

His "weakness" gives him the opportunity to go around the country, sharing with thousands of people his story and the lessons God has taught him. He has had the opportunity to touch more lives than he ever could have in playing twenty years in the big leagues! If during Ed's speaking one person comes to trust God, he says every challenge he has faced is made worth the suffering: "There's a price to pay for success in life, and you have to face life's challenges head on. We learn and grow from each of life's curves, so that we can be all that God intended for us."

His physical body is now eighty pounds heavier thanks to the transplant and the drugs he takes. But he just laughs about his change in appearance, delighting his audience by quipping that "a waist is a terrible thing to mind!" He encourages people to "lace up and shine your shoes, and step into the batter's box of life" so they can "keep swinging for life's fences." This is baseball talk for trusting that God will be right behind you all the way to the winners' circle!

—————— ANGEL REFLECTIONS AND ACTIONS ——————

Reflection In the last few years, where have you placed your trust?

Action Write on a sheet of paper three big challenges you have faced and overcome within the last year. Below each challenge, write the nature of the trust you developed to come through it. For example, one of your challenges might be finding time for yourself or your family. As one employee discovered when she faced this challenge, she could leave earlier if she just gave herself permission. What trusting belief did she develop? It was the belief that she has given a good, full day's work and is justified in leaving at a reasonable hour. A year later, after trusting her decision, this employee is still very happy; she enjoys a more balanced workday, and her employer has a happier, more productive employee.

Angel Advice Corner

Bringing More Trust into Your Workplace

Here are some simple tips for bringing more trust into your workplace. Review them regularly for further direction in building the power of trust in your world of work.

- *Be consistent.* It is very difficult to build trust if you behave one way at one time and another way at others.

- *Share information.* Success today depends on sharing information with everyone. Be the first to share information. If you start sharing, you will find that people share back with you. In time, people will come to trust you as a giver and give to you. Eventually, you will find yourself not knowing whether you give more than you receive.

- *Trust yourself.* To do this better, let the human dust bowl of thoughts that whirl through your mind settle down. Take time to just do nothing. M. Scott Peck was once asked how he accomplished so much. His answer was simply that for two hours each day he did nothing. In other words, he trusted himself enough to know that if he let the maelstrom of thoughts calm down daily, he would see more clearly the few things he needed to do to be most successful. He also saw that spending time on people, building trust, is more important than spending time on "things."

- *Build trust at all organizational levels.* In most organizations, goals are established at the top and then handed down. People feel no commitment to them because they have not been involved in establishing them. You can intuit how this policy does not work in an empowered workplace. To break down the traditional, hierarchically reinforced belief that all the brains are at the top of the organization, you have to build trust first.

- *Create open dialogue sessions.* Building or rebuilding trust among peers is one of the greatest challenges businesses face today. Downsizing has taken its toll psychologically on workers' trust. Employees often become territorial, wondering whether they need to work to protect their own jobs or whether it is their colleagues' jobs that are in the most jeopardy. Either way, they lose. Recognizing this fact and hosting open dialogue sessions to release past pains and future fears can go a long way in rebuilding workplace trust.

- *Build trust by building knowledge.* Because of everyone feeling themselves to be responsible and acting on their own, organizations need to set up systems to effectively build a knowledge base of people's specialized skills and knowledge. Yet trust must come first, or accumulated knowledge will never be as rich as it could be. Therefore, take time to find areas in which your organization is currently in a "trust deficit." Build trust capital by addressing rather than avoiding the problem. Move from a state of awareness to development of a process that addresses trust issues.

- *Clarify fundamental beliefs, and then translate them into commonly held, agreed-upon values.* The validation process that follows clarification aligns others with the company's values.

- *Practice multidimensional listening.* From Eileen McDargh comes this idea. "Multidimensional listening is the cornerstone for self-trust. There is the first dimension of becoming quiet, reflective, and listening to that still voice inside each one of us that tells us not only who we are but who we can be. It is the dimension of being open to the feedback of others, willing to hear the feedback we might not like but need to hear. It is the dimension of listening to the intellect that tells us all the ways in which we can learn and practice our specific skills. It is in practice that we become comfortable and begin to trust our own abilities. In the Talmud, it is written that for every blade of grass, there is an angel bending over it, whispering 'Grow, grow.' If an angel bends over grass, how much more does an angel bend over all of us, whispering 'Grow, grow.'"

Trust: A Summary of Angel Actions

Build trust by finding people with similar values. Whereas your interests change continually, your values tend to remain fairly constant. You will find that special angel alliances with individuals who hold similar values help you become a better person and leader. Write your three most important values or beliefs. How does trust relate to them? For example, suppose your first value is excellence; trust in yourself and others is essential to achieving above-average results.

Create a code of conduct for your workplace based on trust. Include, for example, statements such as

- Management doesn't play favorites.
- Our opinions are considered.
- We are kept informed about significant matters having an impact on our company and our work.
- Differences are valued.
- We listen to each other.

Identify someone in your workplace you can turn to as a role model for building trust. In advance of a face-to-face meeting, write the three things that you would most like to learn from the person. Ask to spend just fifteen minutes twice a month talking about these three things. With time, add to your list new ideas about learning to trust, and share them during your meetings.

Write five things you have done in the last month to build trust in your workplace. Next, write five other things you will do to build trust in the next thirty days. The process of building trust creates more trusting relationships in your life, and subsequently more satisfaction.

Get involved with an organization like the Girl Scouts. There are many organizations looking for angels in the workplace. Ask your colleagues and friends, "Who do you know who is truly enjoying their volunteer work?" Then go out and volunteer for those organizations. They are the ones that understand what a gift a volunteer is; these are the places where you fully embrace the benefits of being a successful volunteer.

Write on a sheet of paper three big challenges you have faced and overcome within the last year. Below each challenge, write the nature of the trust you developed to come through it.

LOVE

*Caring Deeply and
Expressing That Caring for Others*

*There is more hunger for love and appreciation in this world
than for bread.*

—MOTHER TERESA

L ove may seem to be the most difficult angel belief to ac-
quire. Many people view love as personal and familial, in-
appropriate for a workplace. Some portion it out in small
spoonfuls, feeling it is too precious and rare to give freely.

All of us, however, have an inexhaustible supply of love to
give, and we can do so as appropriately in a workplace setting as
anywhere else. We can express our caring for bosses, subordinates, suppliers, customers, and all the other people we work
with, without being gushy or maudlin. At its essence, love in the
workplace describes a word or deed that expresses caring beyond
the call of duty. It means caring enough to take the time to develop an understanding of the needs of those you work with
every day. Instead of asking someone who has just returned to
work after a serious illness how she is, you take the time to let
her talk about her illness; you volunteer to help her catch up
with her work; you offer to drive her home, to listen to her complain about her doctor, and to share your empathy for her plight.

All this takes effort. It is difficult to get past the fear and
embarrassment that prohibit many of us from being loving
bosses and employees. But if we can get past it, there is a

tremendous payoff. Certainly there is great satisfaction in seeing how a loving gesture makes other people glow; it is amazing how a genuinely caring boss can earn people's loyalty and
respect faster and better than one who uses threats and emo-
tionless incentives.

But there is another reward, equally effective. Love does
not just light up others in the workplace; it lights *us* up if we
give it freely and unconditionally. When we give love, we demonstrate to ourselves that we are good people. It is one thing
to think *I really like my team; I wish there were something I could
do to show them how much I value and respect them.* It is another
to write a letter to the team and explain how much they mean
to you, both as individuals and in terms of achieving work
goals. We can talk all we want about doing pro bono work, but
when we actually make a commitment to help a group we really care about, it is uplifting. I cannot tell you how many people have confessed to me how ebullient they became after a
loving workplace act. As one person put it: "I grew up in a
business environment where open expressions of caring were
viewed either as weakness or as buttering up the boss. To tell
my group that they really were important to me, both personally and professionally, was difficult. But when I did so, I
felt lighter, as if I had shed some enormous burden."

Workplace angels show their love for others in countless
ways, as the stories in this chapter make clear. Sometimes the
expression is as simple as providing supportive forums for people to air their personal and professional concerns. Other times
it is sitting down with someone who is troubled and just listening to him talk about his fears. There are instances where
we give love the form of an action, program, or policy that
makes things easier for those we care about.

All of these types of love are *expressed* in words and deeds.
This is the key word that separates workplace angels from others. Angels find original and meaningful ways to express their
love. They do and say things that comfort and inspire others.

All of us have love inside; getting it outside of ourselves is the trick. I hope the reflections and actions in this chapter help you find ways to express the love you possess.

The Conductor of Love

In the workplace, what you put out is what you receive. If you put out friendliness and love for other people, that is what you get in return. This is what I try to put out in my workforce for all kinds of people.

BENNIE BRUNSON, *WORKPLACE ANGEL OF LOVE*

Bennie Brunson is an extraordinary workplace angel. As a conductor for the Chicago Metro Railroad for the past thirty-three years, he has been much loved by the hundreds of commuters who ride in his section of the train every day. He is one of the first people they see when they begin their workday, and often the last they see when it is over. His typical day starts at 4:30 A.M. and doesn't end until 6:00 P.M. Making six runs daily can take its toll on even the most pleasant personality. But for Bennie, each opportunity to brighten someone's day is worth the time: "I just try to help others feel good about themselves to carry out their days better. Then they will also pass on something good to others. Everyone is special."

Bennie says his job is all about "serving, protecting, and correcting," and he takes his duties very seriously. He attributes his special brand of service to a deep belief in love. He cares profoundly about the people he serves.

If there is one area in which he goes the extra mile, it is in serving. If someone is lost, he takes the time to make sure she gets to where she wants to go, even if it means forgoing a break or working late. There was the time a middle-aged woman missed a connecting Amtrak train to Milwaukee, which is ninety minutes' distance from the Metro's last stop.

She was upset because she had an important meeting she was going to miss. Bennie drove her all the way to Milwaukee. The woman thanked him profusely for going out of his way so that she could make it to her meeting. When she tried to pay him, he refused politely, saying, "It was just important to get you where you needed to go."

His gift of love through serving has also involved unusual assistance, as when he picked up and delivered income tax packages to the post office for people who were not going to have time to get their returns in by the postmark deadline.

There are also the many times he has served as loan officer, as when a young woman came aboard crying that her purse was stolen and she had no way to get home. He lent her five dollars to get home.

People search out Bennie's cars to ride with the conductor who cares. There is an older man, handicapped with a hip injury, who rides the train twice a month, and a young blind violinist who travels every Sunday to play during church services thirty miles away. Bennie waits for them—"my friends"—to arrive and then ensures they make their connections. One rider commented, "In the fifteen years I've been riding the train, I've never seen him raise his voice in a mean or angry way. I've only seen him smiling and looking for the next kind thing he can do for someone."

What inspires Bennie to share his special brand of love day in, day out? "The Lord put us here for a reason," he explains. "I believe mine is to inspire. If you take a canoe, set it in the water, and put a person in it, someone from the outside still has to give it a push in order for it to get started moving in the water. I see myself as the person who gets someone moving in the right direction."

Faces light up when they hear him approaching. They can picture his smile in the laugh that precedes almost every greeting he gives to passengers. Everyone is a friend to him, not a stranger. Even when there are challenging passengers or those who try to cause trouble, Bennie just lets them know he is the one in charge of the train. He knows how to do his job and calmly but firmly handles the situation. "Each situation is unique, but I make sure I handle each person with respect and consideration."

Probably the most unusual service he provides is that of marriage counselor. There was a couple, two college professors, who rode the evening 7:50 out of Chicago. Bennie recounts the story: "They had had a few spats, and I found myself becoming the mediator and counselor for them. I loved them both and hated to see them so angry at one another." When he found out they were considering divorce, he used his conversations with them individually to encourage forgiveness for one another: "During one of the train rides I had them get up from their separate seats and come together and forgive each other. They did, and then we all hugged." To this date, more than ten years later, the couple is still together and thankful for the conductor who helped them put aside their differences and focus instead on love.

————— ANGEL REFLECTIONS AND ACTIONS —————

Reflection Where are you missing an opportunity to serve?

Action Write the names of people in your daily contact for whom you can "serve, protect, or correct" something in their lives. Beside their names, write one action you can take in the next week to make a difference in their lives. At the end of the week, look at your list. How does it feel to be an angel in the workplace espousing love? Think of the positive influence you have created.

Leaving for Love

I want [my children] to grow up taking care and loving attitudes into their workplaces.

STUART PASTER, *WORKPLACE ANGEL*

S tuart Paster had a choice to make, and only he could make it. Two years earlier, he exhibited all the trappings of material success. He had the corner office as president of a $25 million electronics company, a big house, fancy cars, and plenty of company perks. He also had a wife with her own successful career and four sons aged three to nineteen.

But all was not right in paradise. He was always behind the eight ball. As he tells it, "I worked seventy to eighty hours a week and then worried all weekend how I was going to keep what I had. I was afraid that somehow the next deal wouldn't go through, and perhaps the one after that. In other words, I was always expecting something to go wrong."

He also had to answer to the company CEO, who operated on getting results through intimidation. Stuart reflects: "He had quite an ego. He would introduce himself as CEO, making sure everyone knew he was in charge." Stuart spent sixteen years working for a boss who eventually began to remind him too much of his own mother. "I felt that I could never live up to this man's expectations of me. I now realize that I could *never* live up to his unrealistic expectations. What I did realize back then, however, was that I was beginning to lose my own self-worth."

Priding himself on coming up with positive solutions to address business crises quickly, he tried to use the same process for himself. But he discovered there was no quick fix. So he chose to take an action that surprised everyone who knew him. He left his sixteen-year place of employment and the presidency to make a leap of faith.

Upon his decision to leave, he created a home office where he could find the private time he needed to seek out what really mattered to him and what path he should take next. "I still didn't know what I wanted to do, but I knew I loved myself enough not to take any more personal abuse."

Today you can find Stuart at home taking time to reconnect with his two younger sons, taking them to school, making them lunch, even tucking them in bed every night. He says he never used to get the chance to read to them and now reads regularly. Now he is the cocaretaker of his sons, who are very happy to have their dad around every day to hear their stories about school and to receive extra help with their homework. "I have found myself spending more time sharing my love for my boys and wife. It has been the best healing—better than a doctor could have prescribed. Perhaps, I'll stay here for a while. That's OK with me. I'm in no rush to jump back into the fast lane of the corporate world."

He is now spending his time planning a better way of working. Even more important, he is showing his sons how to become loving people themselves. He adds, "I want them to grow up taking caring and loving attitudes into their workplaces. And my next position? Well, whatever that may be, I will take all this knowledge I'm learning, of how to be loving, with me back into the corporate world."

Stuart's journey brought him to connecting with his core self, which lay hidden while he was working in a place with leadership that did not value loving attitudes toward others. By removing himself from his unhealthy environment, he regained his love and self-esteem. When he returns to the workplace he will no doubt be an impressive leader building a caring workplace day by day.

——————— ANGEL REFLECTIONS AND ACTIONS ———————

Reflection What journey have you taken to discover your love for yourself?

Action Identify a new space that you have not yet been to, perhaps a library, museum, or coffee shop. Take along a journal and start exploring your views on your love for yourself. What is it that you like most about yourself? What do you want to change? Return to your new space often, aware that it has been selected for exploration of self-love. This in turn leads to sharing your love with others, for you can only give love once you have it within yourself to give. Get in touch with that love today. You owe it to yourself.

Love and Shoe Shines

Then he asked the most important question: "And why are you waiting [to show your love]?"

RICK JAKLE, SPEAKING OF *WORKPLACE ANGEL MICKEY*

Rick Jakle is a workplace angel himself. As a highly successful speaker, he shares his wisdom with workplace audiences all over the world. In his own words, here is the story of a special workplace angel he has come to know.

ANGELS OFTEN suddenly appear in our workplace without warning or invitation, and, in my experience at least, without wings, halos, or even shiny robes. They don't appear when we want them but come instead out of the blue, when perhaps we need them the most.

Over the years, as I worked hard to get ahead in business and add to my net worth, often (to my discredit) my focus was on business deals—not people, but on the process rather than the person.

One memorable day, I dashed out of the house, late for a bank board meeting, without so much as saying good-bye to my lovely wife, Sharon. After a meeting filled with all kinds of important business decisions at my bank (I couldn't tell you what even one of them was today), I stopped by my shoe shine man.

I'd like you to meet him. His name is Mickey, and he's Irish. You'll notice a twinkle in his eighty-one-year-old blue eyes. His wings are neatly hidden beneath his plaid shirt, and his halo is not apparent, but it's there. Mickey is an Irish angel.

This octogenarian cherub has shined my shoes for almost a quarter of a century. But that particular day, as Mickey began to shine my shoes, he looked up at me and said, "Mr. Jakle, don't wait to buy your wife that dinette set."

I said, "Mickey, what in the world are you talking about?"

He said, "Me and Lizzie's been married for sixty-one years. When we first got hitched, we had this awful old dinette set my parents gave us. It was solid wood—hardwood, ugly as sin, really uncomfortable. Just about every day of our married life, Lizzie complained about it. I'd tell her, 'Doncha worry, Lizzie. When our ship comes in I'm gonna buy you one of those dinette sets with quilted backs and padded seats . . . and chrome!' But I never did.

"Lizzie went to the hospital three weeks ago. Heart trouble. But the doc said she'd be OK. Her welcome-home present was the most beautiful dinette set I could find. All chrome, quilted backs, padded seats. Had 'em deliver it and set it up.

"That night I went to the hospital and spoiled the surprise by saying, 'Lizzie, I got the new dinette set for you. It's beautiful. It's waiting for you at home.'

"The next morning I'm sitting at the new table, enjoying my morning cup of coffee thinking about how much my Lizzie will love her new dinette set. In fact, I was telling myself I wished that I'd bought it sooner, when the phone rang.

"It was the hospital. They said they were sorry to tell me, but Lizzie had just died. Oh, Mr. Jakle, don't wait to buy your wife that dinette set."

I think about my friend Mickey and Lizzie a lot. I'm convinced that Mickey was a card-carrying, dues-paying angel. His purpose in my workplace that day was to remind me that in our changing world we need constants. We need people. We need to love each other—showing that love daily.

Mickey was saying that we *are* all connected, that we need to maintain balance in our lives by carefully setting our priorities. What he taught me is that if people are important in our lives we should let them know it, make a phone call, write a letter. But we should let them know it.

Mickey gave me something else to think about that day. He said, "If you learned you were going to die in one hour and you could make only one phone call, who would you call and what would you say?"

He let me think about it for a moment, and then he asked the most important question: "And why are you waiting?"

I didn't know Lizzie well . . . but the few times I met her I was impressed with her joy of life.

The last time I ever saw Lizzie, she said, "Kid, hang onto this day. Make it count. One minute, you're waiting in the wings; the next minute, you're wearing them!"

The way I see it, Lizzie knew all along Mickey was an angel!

Rick's encounter with Mickey made a powerful difference in his life. Today he spends a good deal of his time giving back to those in his workplace, his community, and his home. He values every day as a chance to show others how deeply he cares about them.

──────── ANGEL REFLECTIONS AND ACTIONS ────────

Reflection What legacy of love would you like to leave in your workplace?

Reflection What one big idea can you come up with today to love someone in the workplace?

Action Send one card a week to someone in your workplace: a fellow employee, a boss, a vendor, or a customer. All you have to say is how much you care and appreciate that person. One franchise that repaired mufflers used this process with its current customers. Within a few months, they were able to drop all their more expensive forms of advertising because people were returning and referring friends to the business that "cared about them and showed it."

Daily Acts of Love

A little bit of love goes a long, long way!

PATTI ROSS, *WORKPLACE ANGEL*

Patricia (Patti) Ross, a sales operation manager at IBM, is dedicated to sharing her belief in love in the workplace: "I think it's a gift to share love with others. I believe you can learn from everyone. I've been blessed with my life. I was raised with lots of love. I felt special. No matter what faith you are, you can share these simple, timeless truths with others. You have an endless window of opportunity to serve every day.

"It's really the simple things that have the most impact where you touch people. The secretaries and administrators are true angels in our workplace. They are our core. The people who have had the most success in our company are the people who never forget where they came from. For example, the secretary to my boss is wonderful. She never complains. Recently, she had a persistent cough, which I asked her about: 'I don't want to intrude, but I hope your cough isn't serious. Have you gone to the doctor?' She was so grateful and is now quick to help me anytime I ask her for something. I don't help others because I expect something in return, but I certainly appreciate that kind of reciprocal caring."

Patti offers another example of someone sharing a belief in love. It came in a session her boss held for her and fellow team members.

"My boss is wonderful. She is also a strong manager—even tough at times. One management review session, we were apprehensive because of her toughness. But she started out the session in a surprising way. Using the popular fairy tale of Snow White and the seven dwarfs, she asked us to share which one of the dwarfs we were most like. I responded I was most like Happy, which created a response from one of our team members: 'I want to gag!' However, after a moment we all started to have fun with the question, and today when any of us is faced with tough decisions and our tempers rise, we say things like, 'Hey, you're acting like Dopey. Now, stop it!' It really helps break that tension with a little bit of loving jest."

Patti concludes by noting that "we're all telecommuting now from our homes, so we don't have that human connection like we used to. A little bit of love goes a long, long way!"

────────── ANGEL REFLECTIONS AND ACTIONS ──────────

Reflection Which one of the Seven Dwarfs do you most identify with (Sneezy, Happy, Sleepy, Grumpy, Dopey, Bashful, or Doc)?

Reflection As with the deceptive evil witch in the fairy tale, what lie might you be telling (yourself) that prevents you from loving more openly in your workplace?

Action Collaborate. Find the most proactive people in your workplace and form a group to talk about how to continuously improve your work environment. Create ideas that are simple and fun and can be done with no management supervision. One manufacturing organization called their group "the Angel Team" and looked for ways to bring love and fun into the workplace through small, anonymous efforts performed when no one was around, such as putting candy kisses on everyone's desk. Other anonymous gifts included baseball cards with a note on the back saying, "Hit one out of the ball park today!"

────────────────────────────

Love and Leadership

Where you find no love, give love, and you will find love.

—JOHN OF THE CROSS

When Jan Madori was asked which of the seven angel beliefs she felt was closest to her heart, she chose love. She says that although she feels love encompasses all of the other beliefs, showing love is about respecting and encouraging others, never judging but instead accepting. She feels her company, Personal Preference (located in Bolingbrook, Illinois), is a loved-based business that sells art. She encourages diversity and free thinking and recognizes her employees and salespeople for the unique gifts that they each bring to the workplace.

Although she employs 108 people in the office and 1,400 independent salespeople in the field, she tries her best to be visible and to continue teaching respect, encouragement, and love. There is no closed-door policy here. Her fear was that her "company would become so big that it would lose the personal touch that got us where we are." Last year, Jan wrote that her focus for the business as it grew was to create a more loving environment: "Those who are recognized for performing in an excellent manner display self-pride, which is self-love. My first core value is the pursuit of excellence—seeking it at all times; however, my close second is creating a loving and encouraging environment."

For Jan, love means more than just nurturing, especially if a person comes from some sort of dysfunctional background. She adds that some people have developed very low self-esteem; her warehouse foreman, for instance, came from a rough neighborhood with gangs. "He speaks perfect English," she says, "and you would never know he can't read well. I decided he deserved to be able to read so he could go further in the company." So she sent him to a special training program in the evening. She continues: "My executive vice president acts as his parent. When there are parent-teacher conferences, the VP is right there."

Another salesperson, Mary, came from a troubled family and was a single mother at the age of eighteen. For seventeen years, Mary worked as a presser in a dry cleaner's, making approximately $23,000 by working fifty to sixty hours a week. She went on to night school and graduated with an accounting degree. But she found she couldn't even get an entry-level job without taking a pay cut. Perhaps it was her age, race, or weight that people judged, for as she sought work door after door slammed in her face.

Mary was getting very discouraged when she heard about a company that sold paintings and trained people to build their own art business. She loved art and was hopeful when she came in for an interview at Personal Preference. Seeing in this forty-five-year-old woman a person who had all the potential in the world, Jan and her team of trained managers accepted Mary into the program at Personal Preference and worked with her to help grow her own successful business. "If a person has the motivation to succeed, we can give them the knowledge to develop their skills to become a successful independent sales rep," Jan comments. For Mary, her dream was to own her own home. She accomplished that dream and more in less than five years. Today, Mary makes more than $100,000 a year, has a new Cadillac in her driveway, and even has part ownership in my company.

Mary says "Personal Preference has given me a new life because of its loving and caring ways. It is teaching me to believe in myself, and that is the greatest triumph of all."

Jan insists that her mission as president of Personal Preference is not selling art; her mission is developing women. She also encourages couples to begin businesses together because she likes to see a marriage enhanced by a business that they can run together and in which they share power, where neither is associated with a diminished side of the business.

In her own office, Jan tries to keep everyone upbeat and involved; she allows no gossip. She recognizes that people have different thoughts and personalities, and she tries to teach the fundamentals of love, not disrespect or hate, through the workplace experience. But she is quick to point out that she does not allow others to take advantage of her: "In order to create a truly loving and encouraging environment, you have to be willing to confront the few people who try to take advantage of others. There are some people who always have tragedies. They live in chaos. They are always in a crisis mode. To nurture them is not as loving as to encourage them to tap into their ability, to expect more out of them, knowing they can do it."

Two years ago, Jan gave 20 percent of her company to her top managers, believing that if they were owners they would take more interest in the company's future and become stronger leaders. They did. For 1998, sales are estimated to reach $26–30 million. It could not happen to a more well-deserving angel of love.

——— ANGEL REFLECTIONS AND ACTIONS ———

Reflection In your organization, how can you provide leadership that originates from a belief in love?

Reflection Where does love fit in your company's mission?

Action Create a "collage of love." Buy a big poster board or card-board canvas and paste on it a collage of the special greeting cards you have kept over the years from your loved ones and friends. If you want to make it extra special, frame it. Put it in a room where you can see it often, and remember that all the gifts you give others every day are given back to you tenfold.

Angel in the Schoolhouse

Work is love made visible.

—KAHLIL GIBRAN

Allison Pachona is a little angel herself. I met her during a recent visit to her school. She shared with me during my visit that she desires to be a writer someday. Therefore, as I sought out stories of angels and word got around to Allison, she immediately relayed to me some stories about her third-grade teacher, Camille Vena, who definitely fulfills the requirement of an angel in the schoolplace.

Because Allison is an aspiring writer, I thought she should do the honors by writing about Mrs. Vena. So, here in Allison's own words are her insights into a woman who makes her schoolroom a workplace filled with love.

Dear Melissa,

I'm writing you this letter from the deepest parts of my heart. I'm now in fourth grade, and I have a new teacher and some new classmates. We moved up to the second floor. The work is much harder and there is lots more of it. We have to put on our thinking caps and try real hard. Thank God we had an angel of a teacher last year!

Do you remember visiting us in third grade last year? Our teacher, Mrs. Camille Vena, loved meeting you. Joy was all over our room when you sat in our Author's Chair and brought sunshine into our hearts! I am reading and writing a lot these days, just like you told us you do. My friends and I will share our special projects with you when you come back to visit us. Can you read us some stories from *Angels in the Workplace* when you visit us?

That night when my mom told me you wanted me to be in your book, I was so excited! Being in Mrs. Vena's third grade class inspired me to like school. I couldn't have a better career. Then you said I could pick my favorite chapter or my angel story. I picked LOVE, because everything about Mrs. Vena reminds me of LOVE. She loves all of us so much and she is always watching over us. She's kind of like our "daytime mother." She teaches us math, reading, spelling, English, writing, and social studies. But most of all, she helps us stay on the right track. When third grade ended, she wrote us a goodbye letter. Mrs. Vena reminded us to always think for ourselves. She said, "Don't allow anyone or anything to push you down the wrong road in life. Remember Robert Frost's poem, 'The Road Less Traveled.' The harder one is less traveled, but if you have the courage to take it, it will 'make all the difference' in your lives."

Sometimes I listen to the song "Angel" recorded by Amy Grant. The words go, "Angels watching over me every move I make, Angels watching over me every step I take." That's kind of how I felt when I was in Mrs. Vena's third grade class, and I still feel that way when I think about her. She's an angel because she gives us good messages. She guides and protects us. We just spread our wings and fly, just like an angel or a butterfly. Mrs. Vena told me she just loves our enthusiasm. She helps us become the BEST that we can be! School is fun, and we are learning to discover our own special gifts. Mrs. Vena believes that all children are born with their own unique talents. She told me that's why she calls us "little angels." When we look for these gifts in ourselves and in others, and when we love and care about each other, Mrs. Vena tells us WE CAN DO ANYTHING!

Real angels play beautiful music on harps and they sing praises. In Mrs. Vena's class, she plays beautiful music for us every morning when we are writing and drawing. I especially loved listening to the Pachelbel Canon while I was working at my desk.

I also remember how we used to celebrate each other in lots of special ways. Mrs. Vena has a big marble jar in her classroom. Every time somebody made a positive comment about us, a marble went into the jar. Friday was "double marble day." If we received a positive comment from our principal, we got to put three marbles into the jar. After we did so well on our third grade tests, Mrs. Vena gave each of us a gold medal, and she put lots of marbles into the jar. Just looking at the marble jar made us feel special, and we remembered to celebrate our gifts and one another.

Once Mrs. Vena asked us to give oral book reports. We each had to wear a hat while we told our stories. I read "Little House on the Prairie" by Laura Ingalls Wilder. While I was giving my report, I kept switching from my bonnet to my slumber cap. Mrs. Vena like my book report so much, she sent me and one other classmate across the hall to the second grade. We got to share our stories and our special gifts with the other children. That day, Mrs. Vena wrote my mom and dad a note telling them that I was quite a little actress! It made me feel so special.

All year long, other angels flew into our classroom to give us a helping hand. Sometimes they were teachers, family members, or friends. We called our counselor a guardian angel because she was always there to help us, especially when we needed it most. One day we even put a halo and wings on her after our IGAP tests over! Mrs. Vena was teaching us how to celebrate her special gifts to our class.

Every year, our principal reads her favorite story to the third graders. It's called "The Little Prince" by Antoine de Saint-Exupery. Here is a very simple secret we learned from this story. "It is only with the heart that one can see rightly; what is essential is invisible to the eye." I guess there are lots more invisible angels who help us every day even though we don't see them in our classroom!

Most of all, I will remember Mrs. Vena for teaching us that when there are sad times in our lives, we are in a "muddy place." But it is only mud, she tells us, not quicksand. Even though we may feel like we are sinking, like we are on the Titanic, we are only in mud. Mrs. Vena always reminds us that we can ask others to help us out of the mud, and we can help them out of the mud, too. "I will be there if you ever need me," she wrote to us in our goodbye letter.

Melissa, I'm sending you a very special letter Mrs. Vena wrote to me after I asked to interview her for this book. When you read it, you will see how Mrs. Vena helps children when they are in a "muddy place." She can always tell when one of us is feeling bad. She looks into our faces when we come to school. Our angel teacher always helps us turn our sad, heartbroken faces into happy, smiling faces! Maybe you can share her letter in your book.

Here is a special message my mom and I put together. We wrote it to help others remember how Mrs. Vena shows her top angel belief, LOVE. Here it is:

―――――

Mrs. Camille Vena's Recipe for Success

L represents the LEMONADE we can make when life sends us LEMONS.

O stands for OTHER people who help us OUT of the "muddy places" in our lives.

V is for VICTORY! When we try to be our best, and we work as a team, Mrs. VENA says we can do anything! We are winners!

E: EACH and EVERY child has special gifts. Let's help each other discover and develop them, and we will help make the world a better place for all.

Put them all together, and you have LOVE!

Love, your little angel,
Allison Marie Pachona
Chicago Team Member

For many people, love just would not be a belief that they identify with their workplace. Yet for Allison, there was no question that she sees love as essential to her in the schoolroom.

I would be remiss if I did not include Camille Vena's words of love regarding what motivates her to make a difference in her classroom every day.

Dear Allison,
You don't know what an honor it is that you thought of me when your dear friend, Melissa Giovagnoli, asked you to interview someone for her new book! I must confess that I am a little bit embarrassed by it all. I am just a teacher who loves getting up in the morning to see the children and work *with* them as I learn *from* them. I remember so well all the fun we had and the joy in our room when you were in my third grade class last year.

I want to share some of my teacher stories with you. . . .

Several years ago, we had been having a very rough school year with children and their grieving over their grandparents' deaths, and in particular, the death of the best friend of one of the third graders, John. Our class had been following from early in September the sadness of this third grader as he related stories about his next-door neighbor and best friend, Sam, and his battle with a life-threatening illness.

When we had one of our early autumn class meetings, we talked about Sam. One of the kids asked if we could make cards for Sam and maybe John could bring them to him at the hospital where he was then staying. This was agreed upon and the children lovingly made the cards.

Throughout the fall and early winter, we had an ongoing basket for little simple gifts for Sam which the children brought from home. These were sent to him along with more cards and many Christmas gifts of a small nature. Sam loved all this and we did too. We never met this wonderful child, but we loved him just the same.

In January, Sam's fragile body could not withstand the ravages of his disease and he died. John was out for a few days with the funeral activities and saying good-bye to his pal. At our class meeting, I asked the kids what we should do, as I always ask for their opinions and give them choices. They said that now that Sam had died, we should show our love to John. I wholeheartedly agreed.

When John returned to school, he found on his desk a stack of letters from all of us tied up in a beautiful blue ribbon. He was quiet as the kids went up to him. (We had also talked about how hard it was for John to come to school when his heart was broken and how we needed to be present for him without smothering him.)

The next day, I received a beautiful letter from John's mother saying that she and John read and cried over the letters. She knew how hard we all worked on our academic subjects, but that we remembered to love. For this she was grateful, for it helped her child to deal with his grief, at least a bit.

That same year another of my students, Anna, lost her beloved maternal grandmother, who lived next door to her. She was grieving terribly. One day, while I was drawing a line graph on the board, I looked at it and said, "You know, life is like this line graph. Look at the baseline. This is where most of your life falls, where you go along and things seem to be okay." I moved the line up with the chalk. I told the kids that there would be times when we would be way up high, with great things happening to us or just a great isolated day. There also would be times when we would fall well below the baseline, and drew that. These are when you are in the muddy times of your life; you get stuck for awhile in the mud.

I confided that I had been in muddy places as well as in very high times. I told them about some of the sadnesses of my life and some of the fabulous times. Anna raised her head and hand (her head was down during some of the lesson as she was sad) and said that she was in a muddy place right then. She cried and said that she missed her grandmother so much. John joined in as did another child whose father was undergoing chemotherapy. This all led to a long discussion.

I think that this is what life is all about, "being servants one to another." Anna's story has developed one of my own beliefs: being present to others not only when they are in the muddy places of life but through happy times and regular days.

I think that if teachers look at their roles as not only "pouring knowledge into students" but as being a facilitator who guides children to "find out how" and to model good behavior, the entire climate of a school can change. Hopefully, this ripple effect will flow out into the community and on and on and on. . . I am a dreamer and will continue to dream.

Good luck, dear Allison! You have a great future and I will be watching and cheering for you! But remember, today is a gift, so enjoy it and do your best. That's why it is called "the present."

Love,
Mrs. Camille Vena

———— ANGEL REFLECTIONS AND ACTIONS ————

Reflection Think back to your years in grade school. Who was one of your first teachers with whom you felt most loved?

Reflection Prayer: "Dear God, help me find a teacher who can give me the guidance and love that my first favorite teacher gave me."

Reflection Angels give us direction. They bring out our goodness and love. Who brings out your goodness and love in your workplace?

Action Become a teacher to someone in your workplace. Share something you enjoy and are good at doing with someone who does something you would like to know more about. One accounting firm where I worked had "employee talent swaps" every month. They would be matched up with new partners, to learn a foreign language, or improve their writing skills, and so on. Employees connected with each other in new ways can develop a new leadership base for the organization.

Angel Advice Corner

Bringing More Love into Your Workplace

Here are some simple tips for bringing more love into your workplace. Review them regularly for further direction in building the power of love in your world of work.

- *Remember, it all starts with you.*

- *Surround yourself with people who inspire you.* Those people who do not inspire you drain you. Avoid them.

- *Share.* Invite people into your world.

- *Smile.* This shows you are approachable. Keep a mirror near your desk, and every once in a while see if you are smiling. Most people smile only half as often as they think they do.

- *Think of what you have to give.* Calvin Coolidge said, "No person was ever honored for what he received, but for what he gave." Think of all the things you can give. Build a legacy of love that will be honored long after you are gone.

- *Get out of your head and into your heart.* To share love means getting out of your head and into your heart.

- *Create joyfulness.* Gratefulness, combined with love, creates a state of joyfulness.

- *Use the heart as a motivator.* Without the heart as a motivator to do something, you cannot achieve a spiritually motivated workplace.

- *Create a theme for the year for caring more for others.* My personal theme for the last year has been compassion. I keep looking for ways to carry this out in my workplace, my home, and my community. Below, write your own theme for the year (and then post it where you will continue to see it):

- *Get a perspective.* Think back to your childhood. Do you remember what you wore in the fourth grade? How about the eighth grade? If you are like most people, you remember one or two pieces of clothing. Now think about that new wardrobe item you are certain you must have. Are you so sure? Isn't it likely to become just another thing? Yet when you think back on memories that today still hold so much emotion, aren't they usually the simple things like playing games with friends or a loving hug from a relative? You see, it is human connections that hold the most power—those connections of love. So, what can you do today to build one of those memories in the workplace? Try it. You will be glad you did.

- *Write down the traits you love most in people.* What are they? One workplace angel used this strategy continuously and found that his circle of colleagues and friends grows more and more supportive and inspiring.

- *Say a prayer for those people you find most difficult.* Ask for guidance as to how to build a better relationship with them. For example, "Dear God, please show me how to create a better relationship with _____ and _____. Help me love them rather than just tolerate them."

- *Be creative.* Love in the workplace requires us to be creative in our thinking. How can we show we care in ways conducive to improving our environment? There are always ways; we just need to find them. To do so, look at how others are creating love in the workplace. Take, for example, Herb Kelleher, president of Southwest Airlines, who says that two things make his organization profitable; number one is fun, and number two, more important, is love.

- *A prayer for love:* Dear God, show me how to be more loving in my workplace environment, that I might become a vessel offering the one thing we all most need.

Love: A Summary of Angel Actions

Write the names of people in your daily contact for whom you can "serve, protect, or correct" something in their lives. Beside their names, write one action you can take in the next week to make a difference in their lives. At the end of the week, look at your list. How does it feel to be an angel in the workplace espousing love? Think of the positive influence you have created.

Identify a new space that you have not yet been to, perhaps a library, museum, or coffee shop. Take along a journal and start exploring your views on your love for yourself. What is it that you like most about yourself? What do you want to change? Return to your new space often, aware that it has been selected for exploration of self-love. This in turn leads to sharing your love with others, for you can only give love once you have it within yourself to give. Get in touch with that love today. You owe it to yourself.

Send one card a week to someone in your workplace: a fellow employee, a boss, a vendor, or a customer. All you have to say is how much you care and appreciate that person.

Collaborate. Find the most proactive people in your workplace and form a group to talk about how to continuously improve your work environment. Create ideas that are simple and fun and can be done with no management supervision.

Create a "collage of love." Buy a big poster board or cardboard canvas and paste on it a collage of the special greeting cards you have kept over the years from your loved ones and friends. If you want to make it extra special, frame it. Put it in a room where you can see it often, and remember that all the gifts you give others every day are given back to you tenfold.

Become a teacher to someone in your workplace. Share something you enjoy and are good at doing with someone who does something you would like to know more about. Recall the accounting firm that promoted development of a new leadership base by having "employee talent swaps" every month, matching up partners to learn foreign languages, improve writing skills, and so on.

Epilogue
Sprouting Wings and Taking Flight

Give what you have. To someone, it may be better than you dare think.

—HENRY WADSWORTH LONGFELLOW

As we race forward toward the huge, blank slate of the new millennium, we realize we have the opportunity to do things quite differently. We are capable of great things—not so much as a nation but as a world. Whether victim or victor, we all can become the masters of our beliefs, seizing endless opportunities and the incredible power to transform. Using the seven beliefs of powerful workplace angels, we can choose to orchestrate the New World of Work.

We all have the potential to become angels at any time. We are all called constantly; we have only to listen. Abraham Lincoln knew this truth. That is why he asked others to constantly be looking for "the angels within us."

Every time you are called, you have a choice: to be responsive or to be reactive. By responding to your abilities rather than reacting to your fears, you choose a path of leadership and thus influence many through your actions. If you continue to embrace your abilities, your power, you come to realize a deep sense of peace and find order in the midst of the constant chaos of the world.

Are you ready to champion your life and the well-being of others, to do what you can in the workplace to make it a better place for all? Then the dynamic concept of growing where you are planted should be your strategy.

Are you thinking that your workplace is somehow deprived of angels? Do you long for a different place? Start now to make it different. You can do it. It is being done again and again every day, in every dark corner of the world. What makes someone an angel? We have learned throughout this book that it starts with one's belief system and works outward through action. Wherever there are people, there are angel opportunities. May you take flight now, with all the ease and grace of a workplace angel!

Melissa Giovagnoli
August 1998

P.S. We would like to hear from you!

If this book has made a difference for you, or if there is a story you would like to share, please write, fax, or e-mail (preferably e-mail):

Melissa Giovagnoli
2300 N. Barrington Rd., Ste. 400
Hoffman Estates, IL 60195
tel: (847) 310-0571
fax: (847) 310-8386
e-mail: MEGNETWORK@aol.com

Angel Resources and Contributors

This section helps you network with the workplace angels represented in this book. May you and they cocreate angel opportunities that bring into being new worlds of work!

Maria Arza is a public relations consultant. Her expertise includes developing targeted public relations projects, media relations and advertising strategies, and designing and developing local and national programs. Maria can be reached via e-mail at sccarza@worldnet.att.net.

Brian Biro, founder of CLASS (Coaching, Leadership, and Synergy Services), is above all a teambuilder, deeply inspired by an irrepressible belief in people. He helps others tap into their special qualities and capabilities that have yet to be unleashed. As an award-winning speaker and trainer, Brian teaches principles of quality coaching, leadership, and team synergy that make important contributions to every organization and individual he serves. Brian can be reached at 204 Weston Way, Asheville, NC 28803, phone (704) 654-8852, and fax (704) 654-8853.

Anita Brick is director of career and corporate alliances at the University of Chicago Graduate School of Business, 450 North Cityfront Plaza Dr., Suite 340, Chicago, IL 60611. She coaches executives and conducts programs worldwide. She is also the founder of the Encouragement Institute, the Chicago-based visibility and motivational consulting firm that developed and produces the Portable Optimism line of products and programs. She can be reached at (312) 464-8691, e-mail anita.brick@gsb.uchicago.edu.

Bennie Brunson has been a conductor for the Chicago Metro Railroad for the past thirty-three years. With his special brand of caring, Bennie shows up every day to serve his train passengers just a little bit better.

Chris Buzanis is currently interim executive director at Visit Illinois, Inc. She has also held the position of executive vice president of the World Trade Center of Chicago. She can be reached at (312) 494-6742.

Dave Carey is a speaker, trainer, and management consultant who shares his experience of having been a prisoner of war for more than five years. He brings to his audiences a positive and upbeat message about being your best and doing your best. He emphasizes keeping faith in yourself, in others, and in God. He can be reached at P.O. Box 28085, San Diego, CA 92128, phone (619) 485-1530.

Doris Christopher is president and founder of the Pampered Chef. For more information on Pampered Chef, phone (630) 261-8981 or fax (630) 261-8587.

Taylor Marie Crabtree is a socially conscious entrepreneur who, at age seven, set up a business creating hair clips that she then sells to buy teddy bears for children with cancer. She is looking for children who want to extend hugs in their communities. Taylor can be reached at 933 S. Santa Fe Ave., Vista, CA 92083; (760) 940-9302, taybear@bigfoot.com, or www.virtualtoystore.com.

Deborah Dagit is human resources director of diversity initiatives for Silicon Graphics in Mountain View, California. She is a visible and well-respected spokesperson in the field of diversity, and a frequent lecturer on the topic, emphasizing concrete results, employee participation, and open communications. In 1995, she received the 1995 Tribute to Women in Industry (TWIN) award from the YWCA of Santa Clara Valley, California.

Laurie David is an executive at Sara Lee in Chicago, having worked in several different divisions and human resource positions in the company, among them director of employee relations with responsibilities in Central America and the Caribbean. She sees her career as the opportunity to make a difference by serving others.

Bill DeFoore is president of the Institute for Personal and Professional Development. As a nationally recognized speaker, coach, and organizational consultant, he fosters an energized workforce, efficient communication processes, and a creative environment for enhanced productivity. Bill can be reached at 4201 Wingren Rd., Suite 201, Irving, TX 75062, phone (972) 791-0144 and fax (972) 791-0313.

Dan Dickinson is president of General Aviation Services. He is also chairman and president of the National Aircraft Resale Association and offers his leadership as a mentor with Menttium 100, a national mentor program for women business executives. He can be reached at (847) 726-5000 or fax (847) 726-7668.

Karol Emmerick spent the first twenty-two years of her life excelling academically, with a B.A. in math from Northwestern University and an MBA at Stanford, where she graduated in the top 10 percent of her class. She spent the next twenty-two years climbing the corporate ladder, becoming the top financial officer of the $20 billion Dayton Hudson Corporation. In 1993, she felt God's call to leave her position and all that went with it—money, power, status, and respect. Her dreams included becoming a "paraclete," someone who helps others through counseling, coaching, mentoring, and giving a kick in the pants. She currently resides in Minnesota.

Susan Fignar specializes in corporate and individual image enhancement (appearance, communication skills, etiquette, and self-esteem and confidence). She can be reached at 222 Bay Drive, Itasca, IL 60143, phone (630) 467-9200, fax (630) 467-9300, e-mail fignar@enteract.com, and Website http://www.iwwi.com.

Bob Gabrielsen is executive vice president and chief financial officer at Premier Savings Bank. His mission in life is to make a difference for as many others as possible. His bank also holds this mission and practices it daily. Bob can be reached at 1301 Rte. 52, Fishkill, NY 12524-7000, phone (914) 897-7400, and fax (914) 897-7410.

Bob Ganchiff is president of Ganchiff Business and Career Advisory Services. Building on his unique blend of corporate, entrepreneurial, university, and governmental experience, Bob has expanded his career coaching practice to professionals and executives. He also advises large and small companies on succession planning, leadership development, change, and gender issues. He can be reached at 1850 North Fremont St., Chicago, IL 60614, phone/fax (312) 482-8842.

Dan Gilroy is a participant in the Alpha Project, a program for homeless men that puts them in jobs in the local community in Vista, California. Dan continues to make every day one in which he can make a difference in the life of any person he touches. For more information on the Alpha Project, contact Chris Megison, regional director, at (760) 630-9922.

The *Giraffe Heroes Program* is a story-based K–9 curriculum that teaches compassionate courage and nurtures the leader in every child. The nonprofit Giraffe Project also offers leadership training for high schoolers and adults as well as in-service trainings for teachers using the curriculum. Contact the Giraffe Project to find out more about these fine programs and about how community businesses and service clubs can support the Giraffe Heroes Program in local schools. You can reach the project at P.O. Box 759, Langley, WA 98260, phone (360) 221-7989, fax (360) 221-7817, e-mail office@giraffe.org, and Website http://www.giraffe.org/giraffe/.

Barbara Glanz is an internationally known author, speaker, trainer, and consultant with a master's degree in adult education. She specializes in creative communication, building customer loyalty, and regenerating spirit in the workplace and home. She is the author of *The Creative Communicator* (McGraw-Hill, 1993), *Building Customer Loyalty* (McGraw-Hill, 1994), *CARE Packages for the Workplace: Dozens of Little Things You Can Do to Regenerate Spirit at Work* (McGraw-Hill, 1996) and *CARE Packages for the Home* (Andrews McNeal, 1998). She has spoken on three continents and forty-six states to associations, government agencies, and companies both large and small; she lives and breathes her personal motto of "spreading contagious enthusiasm." You may reach her at 4047 Howard Ave., Western Springs, IL 50558, phone (708) 246-8695, fax (708) 246-5123, e-mail bglanz@barbaraglanz.com, and Website www.barbaraglanz.com.

Ed Hearn, a former player for the New York Mets, now makes his living inspiring his speaking audiences to "keep swinging for life's fences." Through years of battling a number of life-threatening illnesses, he continues to meet life's challenges with divine strength. He can be reached through Connections Unlimited Speakers Bureau, 5849 N. Merrimac Ave., Chicago, IL 60646, phone (773) 792-5006, fax (773) 792-0515, e-mail connectionsunlimited@juno.com.

Dean Hudson works for Sensory Access Foundation. Sensory Access is an organization that provides employment opportunities for the visually impaired. With a strong background in programming, he brings to the organization much technical support for the speech software they use as well as lots of joy through his singing (his fellow workers say he has a great voice!). He can be reached at 385 Sherman Ave., Suite 2, Palo Alto, CA 94306, phone (650) 329-0430, and fax (650) 323-1062.

Rick Jakle comes from real-world experience and speaks from the heart. An award-winning and entertaining business speaker, he is a popular and busy motivational humorist. Rick is one of the three youngest national bank directors in the United States and chairman of the board of a 450-bed hospital. He can be reached through Connections Unlimited Speakers Bureau, 5849 N. Merrimac Ave., Chicago, IL 60646, phone (773) 792-5006, fax (773) 792-0515, e-mail connectionsunlimited@juno.com.

Jan Madori is the president of Personal Preference, an organization specializing in fine-art distribution. For more information, contact her at 800 Remington Blvd., Bolingbrook, IL 60440, phone (630) 226-0700, and fax (630) 226-4380.

Steve Mariotti is executive director of the National Foundation for Teaching Entrepreneurship. For almost twelve years, he has been dedicated to providing some eighteen thousand disadvantaged teenagers hope for a brighter future for themselves and the world, through entrepreneurism. Steve can be reached at 120 Wall St., 29th Floor, New York, NY 10005, phone (212) 232-3333, fax (212) 232-2244, and e-mail nftemarr@msn.com.

Leslie Mattison is assistant vice president, business banking, at LaSalle Bank in Palos Heights, Illinois. Her mission in life is to make a difference in the lives of her customers as well as her friends and family. Leslie has been particularly instrumental in helping women create successful careers as entrepreneurs. She can be reached at (708) 923-7042.

Eileen McDargh is a speaker and consultant helping organizations and individuals create work life by design and not by default. She is also the author of *Work for a Living and Still Be Free to Live,* and *JourneyWork* and can be reached at 33465 Dosinia, Dana Point, CA 92629; phone (714) 496-8640, fax (714) 248-7805, or www.eileenmcdargh.com.

Bob Mugnaini is a custodian at a school in his home community of Cicero, Illinois. When he is not coaching, he is volunteering his time to the many organizations where he lives. Bob can be reached at (708) 863-6584.

Jerry Nanna worked his way up to becoming president of Abercrombie and Fitch. He reinvented himself again when he left retail, moving into management consulting and eventually into the financial services arena. Today, he is a senior vice president of a global insurance and financial services organization located in Chicago.

Lindsey Novak is a syndicated work-issue columnist for the *Chicago Tribune* as well as a frequent guest on radio and television shows. She is also completing a book on workplace issues and solutions. She can be reached at (312) 654-9109.

Stuart Paster is the president of S. H. Paster and Associates, specializing in strategic quality system implementation and motivational speaking. He can be reached at (612) 209-0990 or e-mail shpaster@aol.com.

Corla Powell ("Momma Hawk") is founder and executive director of a not-for-profit called Recovering the Gifted Child Academy. It is an educationally based program that empowers children through education and motivation to become productive, contributing members of society. Aimed at inner-city students in grades five through eight, the academy encourages these children to learn and stay in school. Momma Hawk can be reached at P.O. Box 19683, Chicago, IL 60619, phone (773) 534-8800, and fax (773) 534-8809.

Nido Qubein is one of America's most respected professional speakers and consultants. As an entrepreneur with active interests in banking, real estate, and advertising, Nido is also the author of numerous books and audio cassette learning systems. He was awarded the Ellis Island Medal of Honor in 1997 for his significant contributions to our nation's heritage and his outstanding achievements. He can be reached through Connections Unlimited Speakers Bureau, 5849 N. Merrimac Ave., Chicago, IL 60646, phone (773) 792-5006, fax (773) 792-0515, and e-mail connectionsunlimited@juno.com.

Gayle Robison works at Sensory Access Foundation, an organization that provides employment opportunities for the visually impaired. She helps teach Sensory Access applicants how to use braille, speech, or screen enlargement programs at different client sites. She can be reached at 385 Sherman Ave., Suite 2, Palo Alto, CA 94306, phone (650) 329-0430, fax (650) 323-1062.

Mary Rodino is vice president and general manager for central region/national accounts for One-Point Communications and all of its operating companies. She came to One-Point from AT&T, where she was general manager.

Steve Roskam, M.D., is an emergency room physician in an inner-city hospital in Chicago.

Patricia (Patti) Ross is a channel marketing executive, working for Global Small and Medium Business Channels for IBM. She is dedicated to building community within her workplace and serving as an angel for others. She can be reached at (630) 574-4392.

Catherine Sneed, one of the Giraffe Project's heroes, created the Prison Garden Project to teach inmates in the San Francisco jail how to plant and cultivate a garden on the jail grounds. The program has been so successful in turning inmates' lives around and ending recidivism that it has expanded into an outside-the-walls garden staffed by ex-cons, who market their produce to the finest restaurants in the Bay Area, and into the Tree Corps, a city-backed venture that hires ex-cons to plant and care for trees on city streets. For more information on Catherine, contact the Giraffe Project, by phone at (360) 221-7989, fax (360) 221-7817, e-mail office@giraffe.org, or Website http://www.giraffe.org/giraffe/.

Tomasina Stephon is assistant director for alumni career services at Northern Illinois University's Hoffman Estates Education Center. In that position, she has assisted thousands of NIU alumni across the country with career concerns. Although her mission is to serve NIU alumni, she is open to helping other career management professionals as well as individuals exploring how to manage their careers better. She can be reached at NIU Hoffman Estates Education Center, 5555 Trillium Blvd., Hoffman Estates, IL 60192, phone (815) 753-8844, fax (815) 753-8865, or e-mail tstephon@niu.edu.

Charmaine Stradford is a branch operations manager at AT&T. She is committed to giving back to the community through mentoring disadvantaged youths. Charmaine can be reached at (312) 230-6015 or e-mail charmaine_s_stradford@bns.att.com.

Iam Thamasucharit owns the Thai Town restaurant in Stream-wood, Illinois. Iam prides himself on wonderful food, conversation, and great truth. He can be reached at 1036 E. Schaumburg Rd., Streamwood, IL 60107, (630) 372-7200.

Don Vlcek is an award-winning author, consultant, and speaker. He wrote *The Domino Effect* (Business One Irwin, 1992) and his speaking topics include "Why Do We Work So Hard When It Can Be So Simple?" and "Super Vision." He can be reached at P.O. Box 70135, Plymouth, MI 48170; phone (800) 459-0438 and fax (313) 459-1228 or VLCEK@aol.com.

Brooke Wiseman is the executive director of the Girl Scouts of Chicago. For more information on the Girl Scouts, please write or call 222 S. Riverside Plaza, Suite 2120, Chicago, IL 60606, phone (312) 416-2500.

The *Women's Opportunity Fund* provides loans and training to extremely poor women in developing countries to start microbusinesses. With a loan as small as eighty dollars, a woman can start a business and earn enough to feed her family, provide needed health care, and send her children to school. The executive director at the Women's Opportunity Fund is Susy Cheston. For more information, please contact Kerstin Lindgren at the fund, 2122 York Rd., Suite 340, Oakbrook, IL 60521, phone (630) 645-4100, ext. 232, and fax (630) 645-1458.